ECI. ⌐ ⌐ ✓ 5.0

European Computer Driving Licence

Module 3 - Word Processing

Using Microsoft® Word 2010

Release ECDL274v1

Published by:

CiA Training Ltd
Business & Innovation Centre
Sunderland Enterprise Park
Sunderland
SR5 2TA
United Kingdom

Tel: +44 (0) 191 549 5002
Fax: +44 (0) 191 549 9005

E-mail: info@ciatraining.co.uk
Web: www.ciatraining.co.uk

ISBN: 978-1-86005-853-0

COLEG SIR GAR	
Dawson	
005. 52 CIA	

Important Note

This guide was written for *Microsoft Office 2010* running on *Windows 7*. If using earlier versions of *Windows* some dialog boxes may look and function slightly differently to that described.

A screen resolution of *1024x768* is assumed. Working at a different resolution (or with an application window which is not maximised) may change the look of the dynamic *Office 2010 Ribbon*, which changes to fit the space available.

For example, the **Editing Group** on a full *Ribbon* will contain several buttons, but if space is restricted it may be replaced by an **Editing Button** (which, when clicked, will display the full **Editing Group**).

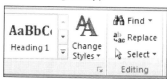 

First published 2010

Copyright © 2010 CiA Training Ltd

European Computer Driving Licence, ECDL, International Computer Driving Licence, ICDL, e-Citizen and related logos are all registered Trade Marks of The European Computer Driving Licence Foundation Limited ("ECDL Foundation").

CiA Training Ltd is an entity independent of ECDL Foundation and is not associated with ECDL Foundation in any manner. This courseware may be used to assist candidates to prepare for the ECDL Foundation Certification Programme as titled on the courseware. Neither ECDL Foundation nor **CiA Training Ltd** warrants that the use of this courseware publication will ensure passing of the tests for that ECDL Foundation Certification Programme. This courseware publication has been independently reviewed and approved by ECDL Foundation as covering the learning objectives for the ECDL Foundation Certification Programme.

Confirmation of this approval can be obtained by viewing the relevant ECDL Foundation Certification Programme training material page of the website www.ecdl.org.

The material contained in this courseware publication has not been reviewed for technical accuracy and does not guarantee that candidates will pass the test for the ECDL Foundation Certification Programme. Any and all assessment items and/or performance-based exercises contained in this courseware relate solely to this publication and do not constitute or imply certification by ECDL Foundation in respect of the ECDL Foundation Certification Programme or any other ECDL Foundation test. Irrespective of how the material contained in this courseware is deployed, for example in a learning management system (LMS) or a customised interface, nothing should suggest to the candidate that this material constitutes certification or can lead to certification through any other process than official ECDL Foundation certification testing.

For details on sitting a test for an ECDL Foundation certification programme, please contact your country's designated National Licensee or visit the ECDL Foundation's website at www.ecdl.org.

Candidates using this courseware must be registered with the National Operator before undertaking a test for an ECDL Foundation Certification Programme. Without a valid registration, the test(s) cannot be undertaken and no certificate, nor any other form of recognition, can be given to a candidate. Registration should be undertaken with your country's designated National Licensee at an Approved Test Centre.

Downloading the Data Files

The data files associated with these exercises must be downloaded from our website. Go to **www.ciatraining.co.uk/data** and follow the on screen instructions to download the appropriate data files.

By default, the data files will be installed to **CIA DATA FILES \ ECDL \ 3 Word Processing** in your **Documents** library\folder (or **My Documents** in *Windows XP*).

If you prefer, the data can be supplied on CD at an additional cost. Contact the Sales team at **info@ciatraining.co.uk**.

Aims

To demonstrate the ability to use a word processing application on a personal computer to produce everyday letters and documents.

To understand and accomplish basic operations associated with creating, formatting and finishing a word processed document ready for its distribution.

To demonstrate some of the more advanced features covering creating standard tables, using pictures and images within a document, importing objects and using mail merge tools.

Objectives

After completing the guide the user will be able to:

- Work with documents and save them in different file formats
- Choose built in options to enhance productivity
- Create and edit small word processing documents that will be ready to share and distribute
- Apply different formats to documents to enhance them before distribution; recognise good practice in choosing the appropriate formatting options
- Insert tables, images and drawn objects into documents
- Prepare documents for mail merge operations
- Adjust document page settings and check and correct spelling before finally printing documents.

Assessment of Knowledge

At the end of this guide is a section called the **Record of Achievement Matrix**. Before the guide is started it is recommended that the user complete the matrix to measure the level of current knowledge.

Tick boxes are provided for each feature. **1** is for no knowledge, **2** some knowledge and **3** is for competent.

After working through a section, complete the **Record of Achievement** matrix for that section and, when competent in all areas, move on to the next section.

Contents

Section 1
Getting Started

By the end of this Section you should be able to:

Start *Word*

Recognise the Screen Layout

Use the Ribbon and Quick Access Toolbar

Use Help

Exit *Word*

To gain an understanding of the above features, work through the **Driving Lessons** in this **Section**.

For each **Driving Lesson**, read the **Park and Read** instructions, without touching the keyboard, then work through the numbered steps of the **Manoeuvres** on the computer. Complete the **Revision Exercise(s)** at the end of the section to test your knowledge.

Driving Lesson 1 - Starting Word

▣ Park and Read

Word is an extremely useful word processing application with lots of features. The following exercises introduce you to the application, to help get you started. There are numerous ways to start the program. The following method is recommended for beginners.

☞ Manoeuvres

1. Click once on the **Start** button, ⬤ (situated at the bottom left of the screen, on the **Taskbar**), to show the list of start options available. All *Windows* applications can be started from here.

2. Move the mouse pointer to **All Programs**.

3. Click the **Microsoft Office** folder to display its contents.

4. Click 🅦 Microsoft Word 2010. The word processing program *Word 2010* starts.

ℹ️ *If Word has been used recently there may be an entry for it in the **Start** menu and it can be started from there by clicking the entry.*

Driving Lesson 2 - Layout of the Word Screen

▣ Park and Read

When *Word* starts, the user is presented with a screen with a **Ribbon** at the top and a bar along the bottom.

⌢ Manoeuvres

1. The *Word* screen will be similar to the diagram below. Check the captions and identify the parts on the screen.

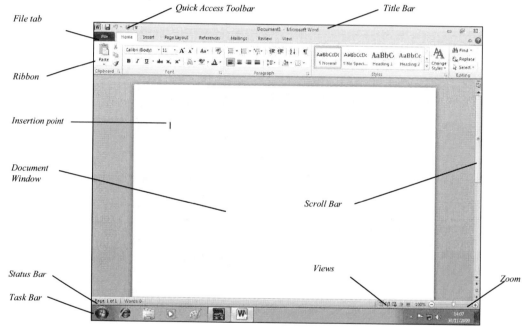

2. The top line is called the **Title Bar** and denotes the application and current document in use.

3. At the top left of the screen is the **File** tab, . This displays a list of basic program functions such as; **Open**, **Save**, **Print** and **Close**.

4. Above this tab is the **Quick Access Toolbar**.

continued over

Driving Lesson 2 - Continued

5. By default this contains three buttons, **Save**, **Undo** and **Repeat** or **Redo**. Not all buttons are available at this stage and more buttons can be added later (**Customization**).

6. Under this toolbar is the **Ribbon**. All commands are accessed using the ribbon. The commands are grouped into a range of **Tabs**, and then into various **Groups** within each **Tab**. Different **Tabs** contain the command buttons for different functions. Sometimes the **Tab** will change automatically depending on the current task, sometimes it will need to be changed manually to find the required command.

7. The buttons are used to select an action or basic feature. Move the cursor over any button but do not click. Read the **ToolTip**, which gives the name of that button, with a small description, e.g. **Underline** in the **Font** group, and sometimes a key press alternative for the command, e.g. <**Ctrl +U**>.

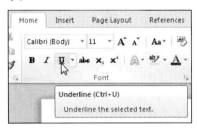

8. The **Status Bar** runs along the bottom of the window. This displays messages as tasks are performed. Check that the current message, at the left, shows:

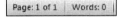

9. The right of the **Status Bar** contains **Views** buttons and a **Zoom** slider.

10. Along the bottom of the screen is the **Taskbar**, containing the **Start** button at the left. The main part of the **Taskbar** contains buttons for each active task. There should be a button there now for *Word*.

11. Move the cursor over the **Word** button. All open *Word* documents will be displayed.

12. There may be other buttons on the **Taskbar**. Next to the **Start** button are pinned buttons to start some common applications, and on the right there is a **Notification Area** which can contain buttons for such things as the **Volume** control and the **Date/Time** indicator.

Driving Lesson 3 - The Ribbon

🅿 Park and Read

In *Word 2010* commands are controlled by a **Ribbon** which is displayed at the top of the application window. The **Ribbon** contains buttons and drop down lists to control the operation of *Word*. The **Ribbon** is divided into a series of **Tabs**, each one of which has a set of controls specific to a certain function or process. On each tab, the controls are further divided into separate **Groups** of connected functions.

Some tabs can be selected manually, and some only appear when certain operations are active, for example, when a **Picture** is active, a **Picture Tools Format** tab is displayed on the **Ribbon**.

In previous versions of *Microsoft Office* applications, commands were controlled by a series of menus and toolbars.

⌒ Manoeuvres

1. On the **Ribbon**, the **Home** tab should be selected. Other basic tabs, are available.

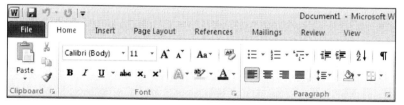

*Part of the **Ribbon** displaying the **Home** tab*

ℹ️ *Any buttons displayed in pale grey are called ghosted and are not available to be selected at present.*

2. Notice how the buttons on the **Ribbon** are divided into **Groups** (**Clipboard**, **Font**, **Paragraph**, etc.).

ℹ️ *The display of buttons on the Ribbon is dynamic. That is, it will change according to how much space there is available. If the window is not maximised or the screen resolution is anything other than 1024 by 768, the Ribbon will not always appear as shown in this guide.*

ℹ️ *The Ribbon can be minimised (hidden) by clicking on the small up arrow located at the top right of the ribbon,* ⌃ ❓ *. It can then be restored by clicking on the small down arrow.*

3. Some buttons produce immediate effects, like the **Bold**, **Italic** and **Underline** buttons in the **Font** group.

continued over

Driving Lesson 3 - Continued

4.   Buttons with a drop down arrow lead to further options. Click the **Select** button, which is found in the **Editing** group. A list of further options is displayed.

5.   Some options will display a dialog box which needs data to be entered. Click the **Replace** button, , the **Find and Replace** dialog box is displayed. Click the **Cancel** button in the dialog box to remove it.

6.   Some groups have a dialog box launcher to the right of the group name, e.g. the **Font** group.

Dialog Box Launcher

7.   Click the **Font** dialog box launcher to display the **Font** dialog box.

8.   This is a tabbed dialog box, similar to those used in previous versions of *Word*. Click **Cancel** to close the **Font** dialog box.

9.   Display the other basic tabs, one at a time, **Insert**, **Page Layout**, **References, Mailings**, **Review** and **View** to see which other commands are available.

10.   Select the **Home** tab again.

Driving Lesson 4 - Quick Access Toolbar

▣ Park and Read

All the available commands are accessed via the **Ribbon**. Above the **Ribbon** is the **Quick Access Toolbar** which contains a few popular command buttons. By default this toolbar has three buttons, **Save**, **Undo** and **Repeat**. This toolbar can be customised by adding further buttons.

⌐ Manoeuvres

1. Locate the **Quick Access Toolbar**.

2. Point at each button and read its **ToolTip**. Some buttons will be inactive until text is entered.

3. The third button is the **Repeat** button. This button has a dual function, it changes to a **Redo** button after the **Undo** button has been used.

4. To the right of the **Repeat** button is the **Customize Quick Access Toolbar** button, ⬛. Click the button to display the menu.

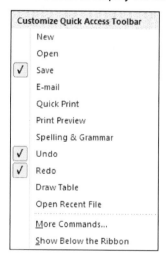

5. To add commands not shown, click **More Commands**. This displays the **Word Options** window with the **Quick Access Toolbar** option selected. This window is covered later in the **Preferences** exercise.

6. Click **Cancel** to close the window.

Driving Lesson 5 - Help

◻ Park and Read

Word has a comprehensive **Help** facility. This means that full advantage can be taken of the features incorporated in the program. Using **Help** can usually solve the majority of problems encountered.

Help topics are available either from **Office.com** via the internet, or from the content installed on your computer (offline). The method of using **Help** is the same in either case but the content may vary slightly.

◠ Manoeuvres

1. Click the **Help** button, ⬛ in the upper right corner of the *Word* window to display the **Word Help** window.

i *Pressing the <F1> key will display the same Help window. The window can be moved, resized or maximised if required.*

2. If the **Table of Contents** panel is not displayed on the left, as shown below, click the **Show Table of Contents** button, ⬛, on the **Help** toolbar.

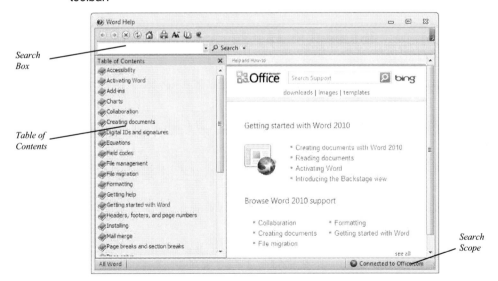

3. The **Search Scope** button at the bottom of the window indicates whether you are connected to **Office.com** or not (offline). Click on the button to see the available options, and make sure **Show content from Office.com** is selected.

continued over

Driving Lesson 5 - Continued

i *The content and appearance of the information provided by the online **Help** system will change over time and may not be exactly as described here.*

4.   **Help** can be used in two ways. You can either browse through the listed topics or type keywords into the **Search** box.

5.   A list of categories is shown on the opening screen in the main display area. Click on any one that interests you to display a list of relevant hyperlinked topics.

6.   Scan the topics shown and click any that are of interest.

i *The same information can be found using by navigating the **Table of Contents**.*

7.   To move back to a previous screen, click the **Back** button, [←], on the dialog box toolbar. You can then follow another link.

i *Help topics can be printed for reference by clicking the **Print** button, [🖶].*

8.   Click the **Home** button, [🏠], on the dialog box toolbar to return directly to the starting help screen.

9.   Another way to find help is to search by keyword. Type **shortcuts** into the **Search** box and click the **Search** button, [🔍 Search ▾].

Search results for: **shortcuts**

Keyboard **shortcuts** for Clip Organizer
    Article | Toolbar shortcuts To do this Press Display the Coll...

Customize keyboard **shortcuts**
    Article | You can customize keyboard shortcuts by assignin...

Keyboard **shortcuts** for SmartArt graphics
    Article | The keyboard shortcuts described in this Help top...

Accessibility Features in Microsoft Office 2010
    Article | Microsoft Office 2010 continues the dedication to...

---

i *There may be many topics found for your search and it will be necessary for you to use your own judgement and select the most appropriate one.*

10. Click the **Home** button, [🏠], to return to the starting screen.

i *The **Table of Contents** can be hidden by clicking the **Hide Table of Contents** button, [🗐], on the **Help** toolbar.*

11. Close the **Help** window by clicking its **Close** button, [✕].

Driving Lesson 6 - Revision

This covers the features introduced in this section. Try not to refer to the preceding Driving Lessons while completing it.

1. Start *Word*.

2. Using the **Search** box from **Help**, find and read the help about how **Add a chart to your document** (use **chart** as the keyword).

3. Return to the **Help** home page and use **Table of Contents** to locate help on **Saving and printing**. Select the **Preview and print a file** option to display the help.

4. Return to the **Help** home page.

5. In the **Search** box. ask the following question: **How do I save a file?**

6. Select **Save a file** from the list and read the help.

7. Close the **Help** window.

8. List the **ToolTips** by placing the mouse pointer over the following buttons (some of the buttons are located on tabs other than **Home**):

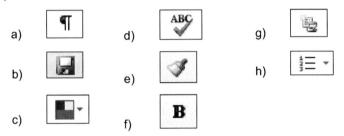

9. Search for **Crop** using the **Help**. Find out how to crop a picture. On which tab would you find the **Crop** option?

10. Close the **Search Results**, then close down *Word*.

ℹ️ *Answers are shown in the **Answers** section at the end of this guide.*

Driving Lesson 7 - Revision

This covers the features introduced in this section. Try not to refer to the preceding Driving Lessons while completing it.

1. Start *Word*.

2. On starting *Word* the **Home** tab of the **Ribbon** is displayed. There are eight tabs by default (excluding the **Developer** tab that may have been added). Seven of the tabs are: **Home, File, View, References, Review, Page Layout, Insert**. What is the other?

3. There are 2 ways to start **Help**. One way is to click the **Microsoft Word Help** button, 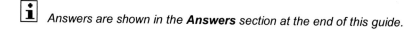, what is the other?

4. Open **Help**.

5. Search for **check spelling**.

6. Click to select the first topic **Check spelling and grammar** and then display the information for *Word*.

7. How are potential grammar mistakes flagged?

8. Search the help using any method to find how to **Add a cover page**. What is the command for this?

9. Close **Help**.

10. Close *Word*.

*Answers are shown in the **Answers** section at the end of this guide.*

If you experienced any difficulty completing the Revision, refer back to the Driving Lessons in this section. Then redo the Revision.

Once you are confident with the features, complete the Record of Achievement Matrix referring to the section at the end of the guide. Only when competent move on to the next Section.

Section 2
Documents

By the end of this Section you should be able to:

Enter Text

Work in Different Views

Open, Save and Close Documents

Save a Document in Different Formats

Save Documents as Templates

To gain an understanding of the above features, work through the **Driving Lessons** in this **Section**.

For each **Driving Lesson**, read the **Park and Read** instructions, without touching the keyboard, then work through the numbered steps of the **Manoeuvres** on the computer. Complete the **Revision Exercise(s)** at the end of the section to test your knowledge.

Driving Lesson 8 - Entering Text

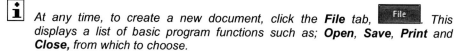 Park and Read

It is not necessary to press the <**Enter**> key at the end of each line as the computer automatically detects the end of a line and starts a new one. This is called **Word Wrap**. <**Enter**> is only used to force a new line, i.e. to end a paragraph, to add a blank line or to start a new line at any time.

<**Shift**> is used to enter a capital letter (or <**Caps Lock**> if a large amount of text is to be capitalised). <**Tab**> is used to advance the insertion point to the next tab stop.

To move the insertion point around a document, either use the mouse and click or use the **Cursor Arrow Keys**.

 Manoeuvres

1.   Start *Word*. A new, blank document is automatically opened.

*At any time, to create a new document, click the **File** tab,* 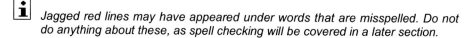*. This displays a list of basic program functions such as; **Open**, **Save**, **Print** and **Close**, from which to choose.*

2.   Enter the following text (remember to use <**Enter**> to separate the two paragraphs):

A computer is an electronic machine that is automatically controlled; it can store a vast amount of information and works at fantastically high speeds. Computers do not have brains, the thinking is done by humans, who feed them information and program them to perform particular tasks.

The first electronic computers were constructed in the 1940s using valves, which were large and gave off a lot of heat. The invention of transistors and later the integrated circuit (silicon chips), led to computers becoming smaller and smaller with greatly increased power.

*This text is saved as **Typing** in the next Driving Lesson.*

Jagged red lines may have appeared under words that are misspelled. Do not do anything about these, as spell checking will be covered in a later section.

Driving Lesson 9 - Saving Documents

▣ Park and Read

If text is to be used again it must be saved. There are two main ways to save a document: **Save As** and **Save**. **Save As** allows file name, file type and location to be specified and is therefore always used to save a newly created document, i.e. a document that has not been named. When a document has already been saved, i.e. been given a name, **Save** can be used to save/update the current changes in that document. If an existing document is to be used as the basis for a new one, but the original must not be overwritten, then it must be saved with a new name using **Save As**, after the changes are made. Both options are available from the **File** tab.

ℹ️ *When a new document is to be saved, selecting **Save** displays the same dialog box as **Save As**.*

⌒ Manoeuvres

1.   Select the **File** tab, **File**.

2.   Click **Save As**. The **Save As** dialog box is displayed.

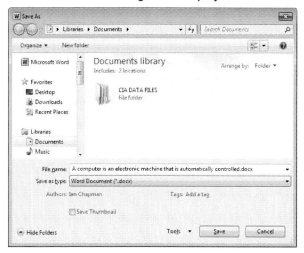

ℹ️ *If a **CIA DATA FILES** folder is not shown as a folder within **Documents** then see page 4, **Downloading the Data Files** to create the folder containing the files for this guide.*

3.   Enter the name of the file in the **File name** box. In this instance, the file is to be called **Typing**.

continued over

Driving Lesson 9 - Continued

i *A file name can be of any length. Choose a meaningful name but do not use any of the following characters: ><"*?:\ /;|.*

4. The location for the save is shown at the top of the dialog box. The **Documents** library is selected by default. To select the correct folder double click on **CIA DATA FILES** to open the folder.

5. Double click **ECDL** and finally double click **3 Word Processing**.

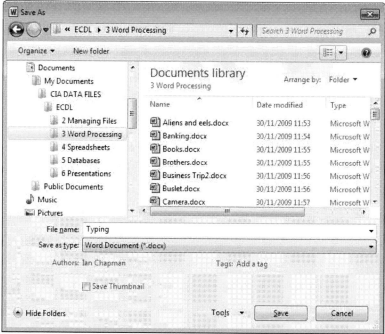

i *If the data is to be saved in another location, e.g. a floppy disk or memory stick, make sure this location is selected at the top of the dialog box.*

6. Click **Save** to complete the save. The file name is now shown in the **Title Bar**.

7. At the bottom of the document, press **<Enter>**. Type in **This document was created by**, then enter your name.

8. You need to keep the original document, so you will save the version with the text added in step 7 with another name. Click the **File** tab then select **Save As**. Change the **File name** to **Typing extra** and click **Save**.

i *Click the **Save** button [icon] on the **Quick Access Toolbar**, or use the key press **<Ctrl S>** to save the document with the same name, to the same location, without displaying any dialog box.*

Driving Lesson 10 - Closing a Document/Word

▣ Park and Read

To clear all text from the screen and begin working on a new document, the current document can be closed. If the document has not been previously saved, or if it has been modified in any way since it was last saved, a prompt to save it will appear. You do not have to close *Word* to close a document, but you should close the application when you've finished working with it.

⟲ Manoeuvres

1. The text of **Typing extra** that was saved earlier should still be present on the screen. Move to the bottom of the document, press <**Enter**> and type in today's date.

2. Click the **File** tab and choose the **Close** command. The following message appears:

3. Three options are given:

    Save   Automatically saves the document before clearing it from the window (displays the **Save As** dialog box if the document has just been created).

    Don't Save   clears the document from the active window, any changes or additions to the document are lost.

    Cancel   returns to the document.

4. Click **Save**. Try typing in some text. Nothing happens because no documents are open at the moment.

 *When a single document is open, clicking the **Close** button,* ⊠ *, at the top right of the Word window, closes the document and Word. When more than one document is open, this button can be used to close the active document.*

5. To close *Word*, select the **File** tab and then the **Exit** button, ⊠ Exit .

 *You can also close Word by clicking the **Close** button at the right of the **Title Bar** and with the key press <**Alt F4**>. If any documents are still open, you will be prompted to save them.*

Driving Lesson 11 - Creating a New Document

▣ Park and Read

A new document can be opened at any time within *Word*. There are templates to create a blank document, or various other types of document.

↱ Manoeuvres

1. Start *Word*. Click the **File** tab and select **New**. The **New Document** screen is displayed. There is an option to create a blank document or a new document can be created from a template or from an existing document.

2. Click **Create** with the **Blank document** icon selected under **Available Templates** to start a blank document.

3. Close this document without saving.

4. Repeat step 1 to display the **New Document** screen.

5. To see the available templates, click **Sample templates** in the **Available Templates** section. Scroll down the available template samples.

6. Click the **Home** button, ⌂ Home to return to the original **New Document** screen.

7. Type **memo** into the **Search Office.com for templates** box and click the arrow to the right of this. Select **Memo (simple design)**, notice the preview and then click **Download**.

ⓘ *If you receive a validation message from* **Microsoft** *click* **Continue**.

8. A new document, based on the selected memo template appears. It contains clear instructions about how and where to enter text.

9. Enter other appropriate text where indicated.

10. Click the **File** tab and then select **Close** to clear the document from the screen. Optionally, save the document if you can see it being used in the future, otherwise click **Don't save** to saving the changes.

11. Templates for other purposes can be opened and used in the same way as memos. Display the **New Document** screen, under **Office.com Templates** repeat the steps above to open a template for **Agendas** and then one for **Faxes**.

12. Close any open documents.

Driving Lesson 12 - Open an Existing Document

🅿 Park and Read

An existing document can be opened at any time, to view or amend.

👣 Manoeuvres

1. The text area of the screen should be clear from the end of the previous Driving Lesson. If not, clear it now by closing any open documents.

2. Click the **File** tab and select **Open** to display the **Open** dialog box. Alternatively use the key press **<Ctrl O>**.

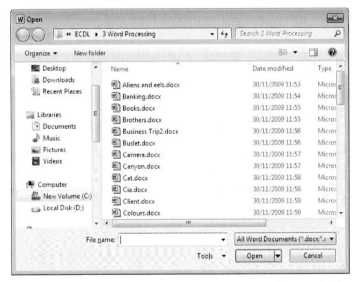

3. The **3 Word Processing** folder should be displayed, if not, refer back to **Driving Lesson 9** for the location.

4. Click the **Views** drop down, and click **List** to see more of the files.

5. Select the document **Warehouse** and then click **Open**. A document can also be opened by double clicking on its name.

6. Click the **File** tab then **Close** to clear the document from the screen.

7. Click the **File** tab again. The recently opened documents are listed on the right.

8. Double click on the file name **Typing** to open the file, then close it again.

Driving Lesson 13 - Views

🅿 Park and Read

When working in *Word* there are several different ways to view a document, they are **Print Layout**, **Full Screen Reading**, **Web Layout**, **Outline** and **Draft**. You can easily switch between these different views.

👆 Manoeuvres

1. Open the document **Warehouse**. This document is in **Print Layout** view, and is shown exactly as it will appear when it is printed.

2. Display the **View** tab, the **Document Views** group is the first on the **Ribbon**. Change to **Draft** view by clicking the **Draft** button.

ℹ️ *There are also buttons on the right of the **Status Bar** to select views.*

3. Click **Web Layout** to see how the document would look as a web page.

4. Click **Print Layout** to see how the document would look on a printed page.

5. Click **Full Screen Reading** to see a view designed for reading documents easily.

ℹ️ *Full Screen Reading view hides the **Ribbon** and **Quick Access Toolbar**. There are **Reviewing** commands and **View Options** still available. Documents can still be edited in this view.*

6. This view has to be closed to return to normal use. Click ❌ Close on the top right. The document is displayed in **Print Layout** view, by default.

7. Click **Outline** to see a specialised view of the document which enables text levels to be easily edited using various outlining tools.

8. Click [Close] to close the view and return to **Print Layout** view.

9. Close the document <u>without</u> saving. An empty area with no open documents should be on the screen.

Driving Lesson 14 - Saving in a Different Format

🅿 Park and Read

Although the usual format for saving a document is as a **Word Document** (with a **.docx** file extension), it is possible to save in many different formats. A document can be saved as **Plain Text** (with a .txt file extension). This means that all formatting, styles and graphics are removed, reducing the file to the simplest text format, which will be recognised by all word processing software. To save in a format that can be read by any version of *Word*, save in **Rich Text Format** (.rtf file extension). Documents can also be saved with a format specific to a particular type of software, such as *Works*.

☞ Manoeuvres

1.   Open the document **Scents**. Click the **File** tab and select **Save As**.

2.   The location where the file is to be saved can be changed using the **Navigation** pane on the left of the dialog box. Leave the location as **3 Word Processing**.

3.   Change the **File name** to **Aromas**.

4.   Click the drop down arrow from the **Save as type** box and view the various options and their file name extensions, e.g. **Rich Text Format (*.rtf)**, **Word 97-2003 Document (*.doc)**, etc.

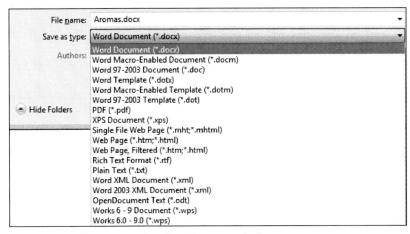

Document extensions, shown above, may not be shown on your computer.

continued over

Driving Lesson 14 - Continued

5. Select **Plain Text** (*.txt). The file name will change to **Aromas.txt**.

6. Click **Save**. The **File Conversion** dialog box is displayed, click **OK**.

7. With the document still open display the **Save As** dialog box again. Use the same data file location, but change the **File name** to **Best smells** and select **Rich Text Format** (*.rtf) in **Save as type**.

8. Click **Save** and then close the document.

9. Click the **File** tab and then **Open**, and make sure the location of the data files is **3 Word Processing**.

10. Ensure that **All Files** (*.*) is selected in the box to the right of the **File name** box so that all file types are listed. Select **Aromas** and then **Open**.

11. The **File Conversion** dialog box is displayed, click **OK**.

12. Notice how the font has changed, then close the document. Open **Best smells** and notice how the **Rich Text Format** has been kept.

13. To save this document with a file extension specific to another application, e.g. *Works*, click the **File** tab and then select **Save As** and change the name to **Works Document**.

14. Select the file type **Works 6 – 9 Document** and click **Save**. If a message about loss of formatting appears, click **Yes**. The document is saved in *Works* format.

15. Close the document.

Driving Lesson 15 - Saving as a Template

▣ Park and Read

If a standard document is to be used many times, it can be saved as a **Template** (**.dotx** file extension).

☞ Manoeuvres

1. Open the document **Winelist**. To save this as a **Template**, so that its basic format can be used repeatedly when stock changes, display the **Save As** dialog box.

2. Change the **File name** to **beverages**.

3. From **Save as type**, select **Word Template**. For the location, click **Templates** in the **Navigation** pane, beneath **Microsoft Word**.

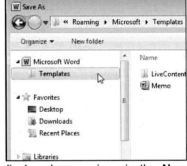

4. Click **Save** to save the template.

5. Close the document.

6. To use the new template, click the **File tab** and then **New**.

7. In the **New Document** screen click **My templates**. The new template is displayed as an icon in the **New** dialog box. Select **beverages.dotx**, if not selected.

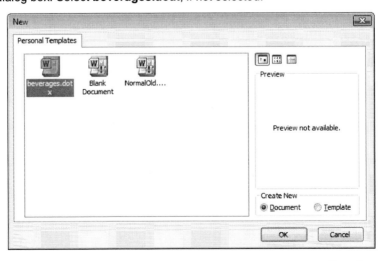

continued over

Driving Lesson 15 - Continued

 If you have used templates previously these may also be displayed in this dialog box.

8.   To open a document based on the template, with **Document** selected under **Create New**, click **OK**. Note that the name on the **Title Bar** is not **beverages**, but **Document**....

9.   Close the document <u>without</u> saving. The template is to be deleted, so that this Driving Lesson can be performed again on the same PC.

10. Display the **New Document** dialog box and select **My templates**. Click with the right mouse button on the **beverages** icon.

11. Select **Delete** from the menu, choosing **Yes** at the prompt.

 Take great care when deleting templates. Make sure that the correct one is deleted.

12. Click **Cancel** to close the dialog boxes.

13. Open the file **Winelist** again (if the location is displayed as the **Templates** folder, change it back to the **3 Word Processing** folder).

14. The director of this company wants to change its name, but is unable to decide from a choice of three possible names. The company is currently called **THE HOOTCH HOLE**. The other possibilities are: **THE BEER BARREL** or **THE PLONK PALACE**. Three versions of this document are to be saved.

 Earlier releases of Word allowed Versions of the same document to be saved without changing the file name. This is not supported in Word 2010. Versions have to be saved using different names.

15. Change the title **THE HOOTCH HOLE** at the top of the document to **THE BEER BARREL** (if you have difficulty with this, see **Section 3 - Editing Text**).

16. Save the document as **Winelist2**.

17. Change the name at the top of the document to **THE PLONK PALACE**.

18. Save the document as **Winelist3**.

19. Close the document.

Driving Lesson 16 - Revision

This covers the features introduced in this section. Try not to refer to the preceding Driving Lessons while completing it.

1. Open the document named **Brothers**.

2. Go to the end of the document and start a new line.

3. Press <**Enter**> again to leave a blank line after the last paragraph.

4. Type your name and the date, then save the document with a new name - **Brothers2**.

5. Close the document.

6. Open **Brothers2** from the list of **Recent Documents** to the right of the **File** tab menu.

7. Notice that your name and the date have been saved on this document.

8. Close the document.

9. Open the document **Errors**.

10. Save the document in **Plain Text** format, as **incorrect** and close it.

11. Open the document **Winelist**.

12. Type your name at the top of the document.

13. Save this as a web page, named **drinks**.

14. Close the document.

15. Create a new document based on the **Oriel Letter** template, found under **Sample templates**.

16. Complete the fields within square brackets with your own details.

 *This template uses **US** date formats.*

17. Click anywhere in the body of the letter to select the entire text and replace it with a short letter of your choice.

18. Save the document as **letter** in your data folder. Click **OK** if a dialog box appears.

19. Add the details at the end of the letter and then save the changes to the document.

20. Close the document.

If you experienced any difficulty completing the Revision, refer back to the Driving Lessons in this section. Then redo the Revision.

Driving Lesson 17 - Revision

This covers the features introduced in this section. Try not to refer to the preceding Driving Lessons while completing it.

1.   Start a new document using the **Blank document** option within the **New Document** screen.

2.   Type in this text:

> **There were many factors that led to the downfall of the French royal family in the late eighteenth century, but perhaps that most often mentioned is the way of life of Queen Marie-Antoinette. Her lavish lifestyle and misunderstanding of the hardships faced by her subjects must have been too much to take for the French peasants, who had no means of feeding themselves or their families.**

3.   Ignore any jagged red lines which may appear under any words which are misspelled, for this exercise.

4.   Save the document as **Revolution**, then close it.

5.   Close *Word*.

6.   Start *Word* and open the document **Revolution**.

7.   Type your name at the bottom of the document.

8.   Save the changes to the file.

9.   Close the document **Revolution**.

If you experienced any difficulty completing the Revision, refer back to the Driving Lessons in this section. Then redo the Revision.

Driving Lesson 18 - Revision

This covers the features introduced in this section. Try not to refer to the preceding Driving Lessons while completing it.

1. Start a new document and enter the following text.

    This year's business trip to France will take place during the first week in August. We will be going to Nîmes in the Gard department, which is in the south of the country

    In our spare time we will be visiting sites of historical interest and a day trip to the Camargue has been arranged. Half a day will be spent shopping with our French colleagues.

    The trip is subsidised - the cost will be £100 and a deposit of £10 is required as soon as possible to secure a place.

2. Ignore any jagged red lines which may appear under any words which are misspelled, for this exercise.

3. Type your name below the last paragraph.

4. Save the document in rich text format, with the file name **business trip** and close it.

5. Start a new document.

6. Enter your name on the first line and your address below, using a separate line for each line of your address.

7. Save the document as a template with the file name **address** to the **Templates** folder.

8. Close all open documents.

9. Start a new document based on the **address** template.

10. Close the document without saving.

11. Delete the **address.dotx** template, taking care not to delete any other templates.

If you experienced any difficulty completing the Revision, refer back to the Driving Lessons in this section. Then redo the Revision.

Once you are confident with the features, complete the Record of Achievement Matrix referring to the section at the end of the guide. Only when competent move on to the next Section.

Section 3
Editing Text

By the end of this Section you should be able to:

Insert and Delete Text

Select Words and Sentences

Select Lines and Paragraphs

Insert Special Characters and Symbols

Use Undo and Redo

Show and Hide Non Printing Characters

Insert and Delete Soft Carriage Returns

To gain an understanding of the above features, work through the Driving Lessons in this Section.

For each **Driving Lesson**, read the **Park and Read** instructions, without touching the keyboard, then work through the numbered steps of the **Manoeuvres** on the computer. Complete the **Revision Exercise(s)** at the end of the section to test your knowledge.

Driving Lesson 19 - Inserting and Deleting Text

Park and Read

Both the mouse and the cursor keys can be used to move the insertion point within a document. Mistakes can be erased, or text inserted wherever required. You can replace existing text by selecting it and then overtyping.

Manoeuvres

1. Open the document **Crime**.
2. To erase a mistake, position the insertion point (cursor) to the right of the mistake with the mouse and click. The <**Backspace**> key (a left arrow above <**Enter**>) is used to delete characters to the left. The <**Del**> or <**Delete**> key can be used to delete characters to the right of the cursor. Make the following changes to the text, using the mouse and the keyboard:
3. First paragraph, first sentence: correct **seet** to **seat**.
4. To insert a new paragraph, position the cursor at the end of the first paragraph and press <**Enter**>
5. Type the following text:

    The identity of the injured man is not yet known but, at the current stage of the investigation, he is not believed to be the owner of the Fiat.

6. To insert text, position the cursor where the text is required, then type in the text. New characters are inserted to the left of the cursor. Third paragraph, first sentence: insert a space in **62Pinewood Close**.

    On making further enquiries the police discovered that he had been seen several times visiting 62Pinewood Close, Adamstown with a man in a Mini. On these occasions neighbours remember seeing a red sports car parked outside. Suspicions were aroused as the owner has not been seen there for some time.

7. Fourth paragraph, correct **fond** to **found**.
8. Fifth paragraph, last sentence; delete the **l** in **managled**.
9. Sixth paragraph, insert a space in **nightof**.
10. Sixth paragraph, first sentence; add **his** between **suspicious of** and **story**.
11. To leave the original document unchanged, use **Save As** to save the amended document, changing the **File name** to **solved**.
12. Close the document.

Driving Lesson 20 - Select Words and Sentences

🄿 Park and Read

Most features of *Word* work on the basis that text is first selected and an action is then performed upon it. The text, from one character to an entire document, can be selected by clicking and dragging. There are quick key presses for selecting words and sentences.

🅁 Manoeuvres

1. Open the document **Banking**. To select the first sentence of the second paragraph, click at the beginning of it, hold down the mouse button and drag to the end of the sentence. The selected text will appear highlighted.

2. To remove the text selection, click once with the mouse away from the selection.

3. Move to the beginning of the title. To select a single character, hold down **<Shift>** and at the same time press the **<→>** key once. Release **<Shift>**. This is easier than using click and drag to select such a small amount of text.

4. To delete words and groups of words, select the text and then press the **<Delete>** key. Using this method, delete the word **Online** in the title.

ℹ️ *Double click on a word to select it.*

5. In the first sentence, double click the word **instantly** in **take decisions instantly** to select it, then delete it.

6. In the last sentence, remove the **as** from **are as careful...** add a full stop after **online**. Delete the rest of the sentence.

7. Text can be changed by overtyping. Select the very first sentence, by holding down **<Ctrl>** and clicking once inside the sentence.

8. Type in **Online banking lets you manage your money quickly and easily.** The previous text is replaced.

ℹ️ *Alternatively, overtyping can also be performed by using **Overtype Mode**. This needs to be turned on first, click the **File** tab, then **Options**, in the **Advanced** section, check **Use the Insert key to control the overtype mode** and finally click **OK**. Pressing the <Insert> key will then start **Overtype Mode**. All key presses will then overtype the existing text until the <Insert> key is pressed again to turn it off.*

9. Select the first sentence again. Remove the selected text using **<Delete>**.

10. Delete the first sentence of the third paragraph.

11. Close the document <u>without</u> saving the changes.

Driving Lesson 21 - Select Lines and Paragraphs

▣ Park and Read

The **Selection Bar**, an invisible area at the left margin of the page, is used to select larger areas of text. Lines, paragraphs and the entire document can be selected prior to performing further actions, i.e. cut, copy, delete or replace text.

ℹ️ *Once text is selected, if any key is pressed, i.e. <Enter>, a, b, etc, the selected text will be deleted and replaced with the key press.*

Manoeuvres

1. Open the document **Planning**. Select the first line by moving the mouse to the left of the line until it becomes 𝒜 and then clicking once.

2. Deselect the text.

3. In the fourth paragraph, place the cursor before **By constant monitoring....** Press <Enter> to create a new paragraph. Remove the sentence beginning **By constant monitoring....**using the selection method above.

4. To select a paragraph, position the mouse in the **Selection Bar**, next to the paragraph to be selected, and double click. Remove the whole of the sixth paragraph. Also remove its title and any extra lines.

5. Now paragraph six has been removed, amend the numbering scheme of the remaining paragraphs accordingly.

6. Delete the last but one line of the document.

7. Select the first two paragraphs by clicking and dragging in the **Selection Bar** (𝒜).

8. Now delete them.

9. To select an entire document, position the mouse in the **Selection Bar** then treble click. Click in the document to remove the selection.

10. Another method to select an entire document is to hold down <Ctrl> and click in the **Selection Bar**. Select the entire document using this method. Delete the whole of the remaining text.

ℹ️ *The key press <Ctrl A> can also be used to select an entire document.*

11. Close the (empty) document, making sure that the changes are <u>not</u> saved.

Driving Lesson 22 - Symbols

▣ Park and Read

Word has special characters (**Symbols**) that are not available directly from the keyboard. Some situations call for special characters, like ™, © or ®.

ᵱ Manoeuvres

1. Start a new document.

2. Display the **Insert** tab and click the **Symbol** button, , in the **Symbol** group.

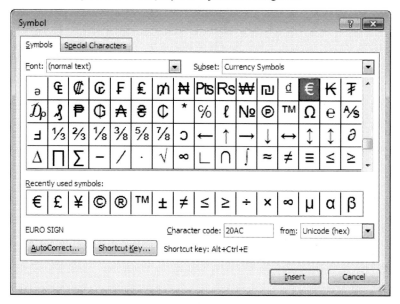

3. The drop down display contains a group of symbols to choose from. Select **More Symbols** to display the **Symbol** dialog box.

continued over

Driving Lesson 22 - Continued

4.   With the **Symbols** tab selected, click the drop down arrow associated with **Font**. Change the **Font** to view more symbols. Use the scroll bars to view all the available symbols within a font.

5.   To position a symbol in a document at the insertion point, either **double click** the symbol, or click once and then click on **Insert**. Select **(normal text)** from the list in the **Font** box, scroll to find ©.

6.   Click on © and click **Insert**. to place it in the document.

7.   A symbol can be double clicked to insert it. Double click the symbol 📖 from the **Wingdings** font list of symbols.

8.   Select each of the fonts in turn and look at the range of available symbols - there are hundreds. Insert a few.

9.   Within the **Symbol** dialog box, there is an option to select **Special Characters**. Click the **Special Characters** tab. Notice that there is a list of **Shortcut key** presses that can be used to insert certain characters.

10. Take a note of the key press for a **Trademark** character, ™ then close the dialog box and use the key press to insert it.

11. Use either method to insert a **Registered** character, ®.

> **i** *To create a key press for a symbol, click the Symbol, then **Shortcut Key**. In the **Customize Keyboard** dialog box enter a key press, e.g. **<Alt T>**, then click **Assign**.*

12. Close this document <u>without</u> saving and open the document **Sample**.

13. Replace all the character definitions (in bold) with the symbols themselves.

> **i** *e acute is the é symbol found within (normal text). Any suitable symbol can be used as a bullet. From the **Font** drop down list, the telephone is found within **Wingdings**.*

14. Use **Full Screen Reading** view to see the overall appearance of the document.

15. Close **Full Screen Reading** view then save the document as **sample2** and close it.

Driving Lesson 23 - Undo and Redo

🅿 Park and Read

The **Undo** command allows the reversal of some of the last actions performed and **Redo** allows reversal of the **Undo**. These commands, **Undo** 🔄 and **Redo** ↻, can both be accessed via these buttons on the **Quick Access Toolbar**.

Manoeuvres

1. Open the document **Camera**.

2. Select and then delete the first sentence.

3. Oops! That was a mistake. To restore the sentence click the **Undo** button, 🔄. The sentence is replaced.

ℹ️ *The wording in the **Undo** and **Redo** tooltips will vary according to the last action performed.*

4. Now click the **Redo** button to cancel the **Undo**. Note that because there are no further actions to redo, the **Redo** button, ↻, changes to **Repeat**.

5. Select and delete the second paragraph.

6. Using the **Undo** button, 🔄, restore the paragraph.

7. Select **Undo** again to restore the first sentence.

8. Are you feeling brave? Select the whole document by holding down the <**Ctrl**> key and pressing the <**A**> key, then press <**Delete**>. The whole document should be cleared from the screen.

9. Click **Undo** to restore the whole document.

ℹ️ *If the drop down arrow of **Undo**, 🔄, is clicked, then a list of the actions that can be **Undone** appears. To select more than one option, drag down the list. Multiple actions can be undone by clicking the **Undo** or **Redo** buttons as many times as necessary.*

10. Experiment with **Undo** and **Redo**.

11. Close the document <u>without</u> saving the changes.

Driving Lesson 24 - Show/Hide Characters

▣ Park and Read

The **Show/Hide** feature allows non-printing characters to be viewed on the screen. This includes paragraph marks, tabs, spaces, etc.

> **<Enter>** is shown by the ¶ mark. This is called a paragraph mark or hard carriage return.
>
> A **<Tab>** is shown by the → mark.
>
> Spaces are shown by ············· . One dot signifies one space.

Viewing these characters can often make manipulating text easier.

⌖ Manoeuvres

1. Open the document **Maneaters**.

2. Click the **Show/Hide** button, ¶ , on the **Home** tab in the **Paragraph** group.

3. Using the down arrow ▼ on the scroll bar at the right of the document, move to page **2**

4. Look for the spaces, paragraph marks and tab marks (in the Conclusion on page 3), as shown in the **Park and Read** information above.

5. At the end of the document, press **<Enter>** twice to start a new line and remove the numbering. Type your name, press **<Enter>** and then type your address, all with **Show/Hide** turned on.

6. Click at the end of your name.

7. Press **<Delete>** to delete the paragraph mark.

8. Notice how the first line of your address now appears immediately after your name. You have merged the paragraphs.

9. Using the scroll bar, move to page **1** and place the cursor in front of **Sharks have no bone...** in the **Body form** section.

10. Press **<Enter>** to create a new paragraph.

11. Click the **Show/Hide** button to return to the normal document display.

12. Close the document <u>without</u> saving.

Driving Lesson 25 - Soft Carriage Returns

🅿 Park and Read

A **soft carriage return**, or **line break** can also be viewed using **Show/Hide** and looks like ↵. Soft carriage returns are used when you want text to appear on two lines, but to be treated as if it were a single line. Another term is **manual line break**. For example, look at the section heading for this section of the guide. This is how it looks in the original document:

Section·3↵ Editing·Text¶

Because a soft carriage return has been used after the **3**, the two lines are treated as a single line and appear on a single line in the contents list at the front of the guide. Had a hard return been used (like after **Text**), the section heading would have appeared on two lines in the contents.

Manoeuvres

1. Start a new document and turn on the **Show/Hide** feature.

2. Type in **This demonstrates soft** then press **<Shift Enter>**.

3. The cursor moves to the next line. Type in **carriage returns.**

4. Now press **<Enter>** and type **This demonstrates hard** then press **<Enter>**.

5. Type in **carriage returns** and press **<Enter>**. Note that **Carriage** becomes capitalised and paragraph spacing is applied.

6. Place the cursor anywhere in the first line: **This demonstrates soft**.

7. Click the **Center** alignment button, ☰, in the **Paragraph** group. Notice how both lines are centred.

8. Now place the cursor within **This demonstrates hard**.

9. Click ☰. Only the first line is centred because of the hard return.

10. To delete the soft return, position the cursor immediately in front of it and press **<Delete>**.

11. The text is now on one line. Turn off the **Show/Hide** feature.

12. Close the document without saving.

Driving Lesson 26 - Revision

This covers the features introduced in this section. Try not to refer to the preceding Driving Lessons while completing it.

1. Start a new document and type the following letter, using symbols to enter the <u>underlined</u> letters:

> Joe's Car Services
> 15 Lincoln Lane
> Sheepfolds
> Norwich
> NC3 1BR
>
> Today's date
>
> Dear Mr Ren<u>é</u>
>
>
> We have just taken delivery of your new Citro<u>ë</u>n Saxo and would be pleased if you could call to arrange collection. Please telephone the number below at your convenience.
>
> Yours sincerely
>
> Joe Middleton
> Manager
> ☎ 0132 5127719

2. Select the third line of the address, **Sheepfolds** and delete it, as this is incorrect.

3. The telephone area code has changed to **0232**. Make the change.

4. You have just heard that the code has reverted to the original. **Undo** the change.

5. Save the letter as **delivery** and close it.

If you experienced any difficulty completing the Revision, refer back to the Driving Lessons in this section. Then redo the Revision.

Driving Lesson 27 - Revision

This covers the features introduced in this section. Try not to refer to the preceding Driving Lessons while completing it.

1.   Open **Maneaters**.

2.   Select the first line of text by clicking and dragging.

3.   Click away to deselect the text.

4.   Scroll down the document until you can see the subtitle **Respiration and Circulation**.

5.   Move the cursor to the left of the document. What is this area called?

6.   Select this subtitle using 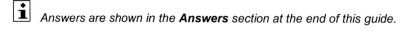.

7.   De-select the subtitle.

8.   Go to the paragraph named **Teeth** and select it using 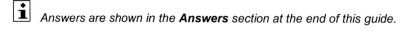 .

9.   Press <**Delete**> to remove the paragraph.

10. Undo the deletion.

11. Position the cursor at the front of the document title and enter **Facts About**.

12. Undo the typing.

13. Redo the typing.

14. Select the whole document and delete it.

15. Undo the deletion.

16. Save the document as **Maneaters2** and close it.

i   *Answers are shown in the **Answers** section at the end of this guide.*

If you experienced any difficulty completing the Revision, refer back to the Driving Lessons in this section. Then redo the Revision.

Driving Lesson 28 - Revision

This covers the features introduced in this section. Try not to refer to the preceding Driving Lessons while completing it.

1.   Open the document called **Frogs**.

2.   Insert a **manual line break** after the words **Common Frog** and before **(Rana temporaria)** so that **(Rana temporaria)** appears on the next line.

3.   Centre both lines of text.

4.   In the second paragraph, first line, change the word **male** to **female**.

5.   In the third paragraph after the sentence ending **do the same lecture next year** insert the following text:

     Unfortunately, they will not be present as two will be on holiday and the other told me he always has to go away at certain times of the year.

6.   Insert the special character © below the last paragraph, followed by your name.

7.   Save the document as **lecture** and close it.

8.   Open the document **Kingtut**.

9.   Turn on the **Show/Hide** feature.

10. In paragraph 2, after the first sentence, enter the following text:

     The dig was funded by Lord Caernarvon, who died shortly after the tomb was opened. Some say this was due to "The Curse of Tutankhamun."

11. Delete the very last sentence.

12. Undo the deletion.

13. Save the amended document as **Kingtut2**.

14. Turn off the **Show/Hide** feature.

15. Close the document.

If you experienced any difficulty completing the Revision, refer back to the Driving Lessons in this section. Then redo the Revision.

Once you are confident with the features, complete the Record of Achievement Matrix referring to the section at the end of the guide. Only when competent move on to the next Section.

Section 4
Printing

By the end of this Section you should be able to:

Preview a Document

Print a Document

Print Parts of a Document

Print Specific Pages

To gain an understanding of the above features, work through the **Driving Lessons** in this **Section**.

For each **Driving Lesson**, read the **Park and Read** instructions, without touching the keyboard, then work through the numbered steps of the **Manoeuvres** on the computer. Complete the **Revision Exercise(s)** at the end of the section to test your knowledge.

Driving Lesson 29 - Previewing a Document

▣ Park and Read

It is a good idea to check how a document will look before printing it. You can tell if the margins are adequate and if the document looks generally OK using **Print Preview**. Print Preview shows the layout of the document as it will be printed.

☞ Manoeuvres

1. Open the document **Retail**.

2. Press **<Ctrl Page Down>** to move to the second page (check on the **Status Bar** that the cursor is within **Page 2**).

3. To preview your document click the **File** tab, then click **Print**.

4. A screen is displayed showing a preview of the document on the right and a list of print options and page settings on the left.

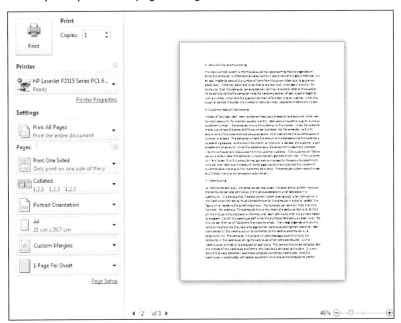

continued over

Driving Lesson 29 - Continued

5.   To enlarge or reduce the size of the text shown in the preview, use the slider, or buttons, on the **Zoom** scroll bar at the bottom right of the screen.

       46% ⊖──○──┼──────⊕

6.   To view more than one page, use the **Zoom** scroll bar to reduce the size of the text until two or more pages are shown.

7.   Change the view back to 50% so only one page is shown.

8.   To move through the document use the scroll bar at the right side of the screen (note the appearance of the page numbers while scrolling) or click the arrows next to the page numbers at the bottom of the screen,

       ◀ 1   of 3 ▶ .

9.   To return to the previous view of your document, click the **Home** tab.

10.   Leave the document open for the next Driving Lesson.

Driving Lesson 30 - Printing a Document

▣ Park and Read

Once a document has been previewed, it is ready to be printed. Various print options are available, such as printing the entire document, printing only a few pages or printing a selected part.

☞ Manoeuvres

1. The document **Retail** should be open from the previous lesson. Make sure that the printer is switched on, is connected to the computer and loaded with paper.

2. To print a copy of the whole document, click the **File** tab and move down to **Print**. The **Print** options are displayed.

3. Click the **Print** button This prints a copy of the document without displaying the **Print** dialog box.

continued over

Driving Lesson 30 - Continued

4. Selected pages of a document can also be printed. Add a number, on a separate line, to the top of each page. Click the **File** tab and then **Print** to display the **Print** screen.

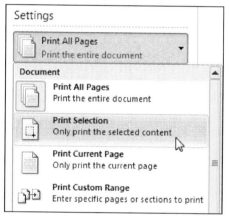 *The **Print** screen can also be displayed by using the quick key press <**Ctrl P**>.*

5. Locate the **Settings** section and in **Pages** type **2**.

6. In **Copies**, located opposite the **Print** button, type **3**.

7. Click the **Print** button to print 3 copies of page **2**.

8. Select the first sentence. To print only the selected text, display the **Print** screen. Delete **2** from **Pages** and return **Copies** to **1**.

9. In the **Settings** section, click on **Print All Pages** to display a drop down list of options. Select **Print Selection** and click the **Print** button.

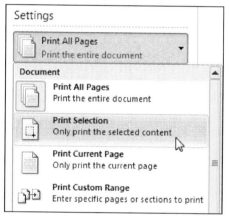

To print the current page, i.e. the page the cursor is on, select **Print Current page**.

10. To print pages 2 through to the end of the document, in the **Pages** box in the **Page range** area, type **2-** then click the **Print** button.

11. Print pages **1** and **3** only by entering **1,3** in the **Pages** box and then clicking the **Print** button.

12. Close the document <u>without</u> saving.

Driving Lesson 31 - Revision

This covers the features introduced in this section. Try not to refer to the preceding Driving Lessons while completing it.

1.   What happens if you press <**Ctrl P**> with a document open?

2.   What is the normal setting for what is printed?

3.   What is the normal setting for the **Copies**?

4.   What does **Print Preview** do?

5.   Open the document **Canyon**.

6.   **Print Preview** the document.

7.   Return to the **Home** tab.

8.   Add your name to the end of the document.

9.   **Print Preview** the result and print out one copy of the document.

10.   Close the document <u>without</u> saving.

11.   Open the document **Maneaters**.

12.   Type your name at the end.

13.   **Print Preview** the document. How many pages does it contain?

14.   View all the pages using the **Previous Page** button, until the first page is in view.

15.   Print only the first page of the document.

16.   Close the document <u>without</u> saving.

i   *Answers are shown in the **Answers** section at the end of this guide.*

If you experienced any difficulty completing the Revision, refer back to the Driving Lessons in this section. Then redo the Revision.

Driving Lesson 32 - Revision

This covers the features introduced in this section. Try not to refer to the preceding Driving Lessons while completing it.

1. Open the document **Pc** and switch to **Draft** view.

2. Select the title and the first paragraph and print a copy of this section only.

3. Print page **2** only.

4. Print pages **3 - 4** only.

5. Close the document <u>without</u> saving.

6. Open the document **Golf**.

7. Preview the document, then quick print one copy.

8. Close **Golf** <u>without</u> saving.

9. Open the document **Maneaters**.

10. Type your name and the date at the end of the document.

11. **Print Preview** the document.

12. Select the section about **Senses**.

13. Print the selected text only.

14. Print pages **1** and **3** only with a single action, i.e. do not print page **1** and then open the **Print** screen again to print page **3**. How did you do this?

15. Close the document <u>without</u> saving.

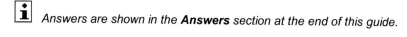 *Answers are shown in the **Answers** section at the end of this guide.*

If you experienced any difficulty completing the Revision, refer back to the Driving Lessons in this section. Then redo the Revision.

Once you are confident with the features, complete the Record of Achievement Matrix referring to the section at the end of the guide. Only when competent move on to the next Section.

Section 5
Formatting Text

By the end of this Section you should be able to:

Underline, Embolden and Italicise Text

Change Fonts and Text Size

Apply Text Effects, Subscript and Superscript

Use the Format Painter

Cut, Copy and Paste

To gain an understanding of the above features, work through the **Driving Lessons** in this **Section**.

For each **Driving Lesson**, read the **Park and Read** instructions, without touching the keyboard, then work through the numbered steps of the **Manoeuvres** on the computer. Complete the **Revision Exercise(s)** at the end of the section to test your knowledge.

Driving Lesson 33 - Underline, Bold and Italic

▣ Park and Read

As text is entered into a document, it is possible to format it as it is typed. Formatting features can be applied from the keyboard, or by clicking command buttons on the **Ribbon**.

⌒ Manoeuvres

1. Start a new document.

2. Practise activating the features using the mouse. Click once on each of the **Bold**, **Italic** and **Underline** buttons, **B** *I* **U** , on the **Home** tab in the **Font** group. When a particular feature is in operation, the button on the **Ribbon** has an orange background. Turn the selected feature off by clicking once more on the button.

3. Practise activating, bold, italic and underline features using the key presses <**Ctrl B**>, <**Ctrl I**> and <**Ctrl U**> respectively. Turn the features off by pressing <**Ctrl Spacebar**>, or repeat the key press.

4. Type in the following text using **Bold**, **Underline** and **Italic**, turning the features on and off as required.

    <u>**Floppy Disks**</u>

    Before a disk can be used it needs to be ***formatted*** which means that the **tracks** on which the computer stores its data need to be put on the disk. Different computers **format disks** in different ways. Personal computers (PCs) all format disks in the same way, making them <u>compatible with other machines</u>.

    It is easy to damage a disk <u>so be careful</u>. Some of the things that can **cause damage** include exposing the disk to sunlight, magnets or moisture, damaging the casing or touching the inner disk film.

5. When finished, scroll back through the text using the left arrow key. Note that the **Underline**, **Bold** and **Italic** buttons on the toolbar have coloured shading when they are activated and normal where they are not.

6. Save the document as **disks**.

7. Print a copy of the document and then close it.

Driving Lesson 34 - Formatting of Selected Text

▣ Park and Read

Text formats are usually applied after text has been typed. This speeds up text entry and formatting. To change the appearance of text that has already been entered, first select the text using the mouse and then apply the formatting feature.

↷ Manoeuvres

1.   Open the document **Parts**.

2.   Use click and drag to select the title. Click the **Underline** button to apply an underline to the selected text.

3.   Underline the three sub headings in the same way.

4.   To apply a formatting feature to a single word, position the cursor within the word and apply the required format. Click anywhere in the text **CPU** in the first paragraph and click the **Bold** button to make the whole word **bold**.

5.   Change the formatting of the following words to **bold**:

      First paragraph: **Control Unit**, **Memory**, **ROM**, **RAM**, and **Arithmetic Unit**.

      Second paragraph: **keyboards**.

      Third paragraph: **monitor** (twice).

6.   Save the document as **Parts2**.

7.   Remove the underlining from the title and return the word **keyboards** to its normal appearance.

8.   Italicise the word **brain** in the first paragraph by placing the cursor within the word, and then click the **Italic** button, $\boxed{I}$.

9.   Italicise the whole of the second paragraph.

10.   Preview the document.

11.   Continue to experiment with the appearance of the document. For instance, try applying several of the formatting features at the same time.

12.   Close the document without saving the changes.

Driving Lesson 35 - Fonts and Text Size

▣ Park and Read

A font is a type or style of print. Examples of fonts are Courier, Times New Roman, Arial, etc. A combination of the software in use and the selected printer determines which fonts are available for use. You can choose a font before starting to type, or you can select text that has already been entered and then change the font. The size of the font can also be changed. *Word* defines size in **points** - the larger the point size, the larger the character appears.

⌒ Manoeuvres

1. Open the document **Fonts**.

2. Select the first line of text and drop down the **Font** list from the **Font** box, Calibri (Body) ▾ , on the **Home** tab of the **Ribbon**.

3. As the cursor moves down the font list the text is displayed in the highlighted font.

4. Select the appropriate font (**Algerian**) from the list.

5. Continue to change the fonts to those stated.

ⓘ *To change the font of a single word, position the cursor within the word and choose the required font.*

6. Print a copy, before closing the document <u>without</u> saving.

7. Open the document **Sizes**. Select each line of text in turn that describes a different size and from the **Size** box, 12 ▾ , choose the size that the text describes. The font size changes automatically as the cursor moves over each size.

8. Try placing the cursor within a word and changing the font size.

9. When all the text has been correctly sized, **Print Preview** the document to see the result.

10. Save the document as **new text sizes**, then close it.

ⓘ *There is also a floating formatting toolbar available, when text is selected.*

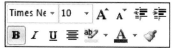

Driving Lesson 36 - Changing Text Appearance

▣ Park and Read

Different colours can be applied to text, making it more eye-catching. Think carefully, though, before using too much colour. It might make a document more difficult to read, or detract from its purpose.

☞ Manoeuvres

1. Open the document **Colours**. Select the text **This text is red**.

2. Form the **Home** tab, click the **Font Color** button, ⟨A ▾⟩ (the button is red by default, another colour may be displayed if the feature has been used already in this working session).

3. A different colour text colour can be added using the drop down arrow to the right of the **Font Color** button, ⟨A ▾⟩. Select the next line and use the drop down on the button.

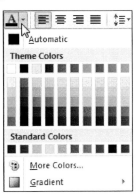

4. Change the colour of the selected text to **blue**.

5. Change the colour of the remaining text as stated in each line (use a light tint of red for pink and aqua for turquoise, the others are selected from **Standard Colors** or **Theme Colors**).

6. Click the **Font Color** button and type your name at the bottom of the document. The text is the same as the colour shown on the button.

7. Now **Preview** your document to see the results. If a colour printer is available print a copy of the document.

8. Save this document as **Colours2**.

9. Close the document.

Driving Lesson 37 - Subscript and Superscript

Park and Read

^{Superscript} and $_{subscript}$ make the text respectively higher or lower than the other text on the same line, e.g. in mathematical or chemical terms.

Manoeuvres

1.   Start a new document.

2.   Type in the following text: **The chemical symbol for water is H2O.**

3.   Select the **2** and then click the **Subscript** button, $\boxed{\mathbf{x_2}}$ in the **Font** group.

> The chemical symbol for water is H_2O.

4.   With the cursor at the end of the sentence, press **<Enter>** and type **43 = 64**.

5.   This is obviously incorrect. Select the **3** and click the **Superscript** button, $\boxed{\mathbf{x^2}}$. The calculation is now correct: 4 cubed = 64, i.e. 4x4x4=64

> The chemical symbol for water is H_2O.
> $4^3 = 64$.

6.   Start a new line and type in the following text: **1st 2nd 3rd 4th 5th**. Notice how the superscript feature is automatically activated by *Word*.

7.   Close the document <u>without</u> saving.

Driving Lesson 38 - Changing Case

▣ Park and Read

Four different text cases can be used within *Word*. These are:

Sentence case	the first letter of the sentence is uppercase.
lowercase	all the letters are in small case.
UPPERCASE	all the letters are capitalised.
Capitalize Each Word	all words begin with an uppercase letter.

There is a fifth option:

tOGGLE cASE	that converts every character to the opposite of what it is, lowercase to uppercase and vice-versa.

⌒ Manoeuvres

1. In a new document, type **the bus was late every morning**. Notice that the first letter is capitalised automatically.

2. Select the text, then click the **Change Case** button, Aa ▾, in the **Font** group to display the **Change Case** drop down menu.

3. Select **UPPERCASE**. All the text is capitalised.

4. With the text selected, click Aa ▾, and select **lowercase**.

5. With the text selected, click Aa ▾, and select **Capitalize Each Word**.

6. With the text selected, click Aa ▾, and select **tOGGLE cASE**. The case of each character is reversed.

7. With the text selected, click Aa ▾, and select **Sentence case**.

ℹ️ *The key press <**Shift F3**> rotates between some of the available options.*

8. Close the document <u>without</u> saving.

Driving Lesson 39 - Format Painter

▣ Park and Read

Once part of a document has been formatted you may wish to use the same format on another part of a document. This can be done using the **Format Painter**, which will copy the formatting applied to the original text and apply it to other text.

↱ Manoeuvres

1. Open the document **Scents** and select the first paragraph. Make it underlined, bold and change the **Font** to any other.

2. With the newly formatted paragraph selected, from the **Clipboard** group on the **Home** tab, click the **Format Painter** button, ⟦⬦⟧. The mouse pointer changes to a paintbrush ⟦⬦I⟧.

3. Click and drag to select the second paragraph. Once the mouse has been released, the paragraph will be formatted in the same manner.

ℹ️ *To format more than one selection, **double click** the **Format Painter** button. This will allow text to be selected in several different areas of the document. Click the **Format Painter** button again, or press the <**Esc**> key to turn it off.*

4. The mouse pointer returns to its normal state, **Format Painter** is turned off.

5. Close the document <u>without</u> saving.

Driving Lesson 40 - Cut, Copy and Paste

⊞ Park and Read

The **Cut**, **Copy** and **Paste** commands allow text to be moved around a document, from one place to another, quickly and easily. When text is cut, it is removed from its original location; when copied, the original is untouched. When copied or cut, text is placed in a temporary storage area known as the **Clipboard**. Up to **24** cut or copied items can be held on the **Clipboard**.

⌒ Manoeuvres

1. Open the document **Planning**. Click the **Clipboard** dialog box launcher to the right of the **Clipboard** group name, Clipboard ⊡ on the **Home** tab to view the **Clipboard Task Pane**. Because the **Clipboard** is shared between all *Office* applications, there may already be some items on it. If so, click the **Clear All** button, ✕ Clear All .

2. Highlight the title **Production Planning** and its associated paragraph. Click the **Cut** button, ✂ from the **Clipboard** group of the **Home** tab.

3. To place the paragraph of text which is now in the **Clipboard** at the end of the document, move the cursor to the correct position, press <**Enter**> as required to separate the paragraphs and click the **Paste** button, ⧉ (be careful not to click the text **Paste** or the drop down arrow, as this displays the **Paste** options).

ℹ️ *Using key presses:* **Cut** *is* **<Ctrl X>**, **Copy** *is* **<Ctrl C>**, **Paste** *is* **<Ctrl V>**.

4. Create another new line at the end of the document, then click the paragraph as it appears on the **Clipboard Task Pane**. This also pastes the paragraph into the document. **Undo** the last action.

5. Highlight paragraph number 7, including its title. Click **Copy**, ⧉ and this item appears on the **Clipboard**, above the item cut earlier.

6. Paste paragraph 7 at the top of the document, ignore the **Paste Options Smart Tag**, ⧉ (Ctrl) ▾ , that may appear after it, then delete the original paragraph.

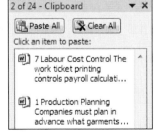

7. Use **Cut, Copy** and **Paste** to reverse the order of the paragraphs so that the order reads 7, 6, 5, 4, 3, 2, 1. Delete the paragraph numbers and space the paragraphs as necessary. Clear the **Clipboard** and close it.

8. Save the document as **Planning2** and close it.

Driving Lesson 41 - Revision

This covers the features introduced in this section. Try not to refer to the preceding Driving Lessons while completing it.

1. What effects do the following buttons have if clicked when text is selected:

    a) **B** ?   b) *I* ?   c) <u>U</u> ?

2. What is a **Font**?

3. Open the document **Food Chain** and apply **Bold** and **Underline** formatting to the title.

4. Increase the font size of the title to **14pt**.

5. Apply **Italic** formatting to the words **An example is:**

6. Apply **Bold** formatting to the line **Dandelion - rabbit - fox** and insert a blank line below it.

7. Apply **Italic** formatting to the words **Other examples of food chains are:**.

8. Apply **Bold** formatting to the remaining three lines of text.

9. Print one copy of the document, then close it <u>without</u> saving.

10. Open the document **Maneaters**, change the font size of the title to **26pt**.

11. Change the subheadings to **18pt**, then change the size of the remaining text to **14pt**.

12. Make the following colour changes:

    Introduction heading and text - **Dark Red**

    Body Form heading and text - **Light Blue**

    Respiration and Circulation heading and text - **Pink**

    Teeth heading and text - **Light Green**

    Diet heading and text - **Orange**

    Methods of Reproduction heading and text - **Dark Blue**

    Senses heading and text - **Olive Green**

    Conclusion heading and text - **Red**

13. Change the font of the title to **Tahoma**.

14. Select the entire document and change the colour to **Automatic**.

15. Print a single copy of the document, then close it <u>without</u> saving.

i *Answers are shown in the **Answers** section at the end of this guide.*

If you experienced any difficulty completing the Revision, refer back to the Driving Lessons in this section. Then redo the Revision.

Driving Lesson 42 - Revision

This covers the features introduced in this section. Try not to refer to the preceding Driving Lessons while completing it.

1. Open the document **Business Trip2**.

2. Select all of the text and change the font style to **Century Schoolbook**, font size **14**.

3. Insert the title **Business Trip** above the first paragraph, using the font style **Baskerville Old Face**, font size **20**, font colour **Red**.

4. Make the sentence **The trip is subsidised...** bold.

5. Change the names of all places to italics.

6. Change the title to **Uppercase**.

7. Save the document as **Business Trip3** as a **Web Page** and close it.

8. Open the document called **Typist**.

9. Rearrange the order of the paragraphs by moving the **All documents accepted DISSERTATIONS, THESES CV's ETC** paragraph down below the **Well qualified and experienced typist** paragraph, moving the line of stars with it.

10. Adjust the spacing, if necessary.

11. Centre all of the text.

12. Change the font of all the text to **Bookman Old Style**.

13. Change the font colour of the first line of text to blue and the font size to **14pt**.

14. Using the **Format Painter** apply the first line formatting to the text **DISSERTATIONS, THESES CV's ETC** and **SATISFACTION GUARANTEED**.

15. Save the document as **special effects** and close it.

If you experienced any difficulty completing the Revision, refer back to the Driving Lessons in this section. Then redo the Revision.

Driving Lesson 43 - Revision

This covers the features introduced in this section. Try not to refer to the preceding Driving Lessons while completing it.

1. Open the document **Exchange** and print one copy.

2. Display the **Clipboard Task Pane**.

3. If appropriate, clear any existing content from the **Clipboard**.

4. Select the third paragraph beginning **We will be visiting interesting sites...** and **Copy** the text.

5. **Paste** the text so that it becomes the second paragraph.

6. Delete the copied paragraph from its original position.

7. Select the final paragraph beginning **The following staff...** and **Cut** the text.

8. **Paste** the text so that it becomes fourth paragraph.

9. Print a copy of the document in its current form.

10. Ensure that the **Clipboard** is cleared then select the first paragraph and **Cut** it.

11. Select and **Cut** each of the remaining paragraphs in turn until the document has no text left in it.

12. Use the **Clipboard** to **Paste** the paragraphs back into their original positions.

13. Close the document without saving.

14. Clear the **Clipboard** and then close it.

If you experienced any difficulty completing the Revision, refer back to the Driving Lessons in this section. Then redo the Revision.

Driving Lesson 44 - Revision

This covers the features introduced in this section. Try not to refer to the preceding Driving Lessons while completing it.

1. Open the document **Sicklist**. Use the **Cut** and **Paste** command to put each employee's record in ascending alphabetical order, by surname.

2. Make the first six names bold and green, the second six italic and pink and the remaining names underlined and blue. Change the font of all the text to **Tahoma 9pt** (use a different font if necessary).

3. Print the document.

4. Copy all the records and paste them at the end of the document. Change the font of the last two copied records to **Arial** and make them purple and bold.

5. Use the **Format Painter** to apply this formatting to the remainder of the list, then close the document <u>without</u> saving.

6. Clear and remove the **Clipboard** and open the document **Penman**.

7. Move the last sentence of the third paragraph beginning **If you are interested**, to form a new last paragraph.

8. Add in the telephone number **Tel.: (0191) 549 5002** between the address and the date.

9. Highlight the text **Penman Walker** and **The world's first robotic dog walker**. Embolden the selected text.

10. Underline **VERY** in at **VERY low cost** and italicise the word **PENMAN** in the third paragraph.

11. Select all of the text and change the font and size to **Arial 12pt**.

12. Select **Penman Walker** and change its size to **20**.

13. Save the document using the filename **Penman2**.

14. Print a copy of the document, then close it.

If you experienced any difficulty completing the Revision, refer back to the Driving Lessons in this section. Then redo the Revision.

Once you are confident with the features, complete the Record of Achievement Matrix referring to the section at the end of the guide. Only when competent move on to the next Section.

Section 6
Tools

By the end of this Section you should be able to:

Check Spelling

Hyphenate Text

Search for Text

Replace Text

Use the Zoom Control

Change Preferences

To gain an understanding of the above features, work through the **Driving Lessons** in this **Section**.

For each **Driving Lesson**, read the **Park and Read** instructions, without touching the keyboard, then work through the numbered steps of the **Manoeuvres** on the computer. Complete the **Revision Exercise(s)** at the end of the section to test your knowledge.

Driving Lesson 45 - Spelling Checker

⏸ Park and Read

Word comes with a large dictionary, to help you check spelling in a document. Proper names and places can be added to a supplementary dictionary. There are two main ways of spell checking. Either spell check while typing, or use the **Spelling and Grammar Checker**. This feature allows you to delete repeated words as well as correct spelling errors.

ⓘ *To check spelling while typing, click the **File** tab and click the **Options** button, above **Exit**. Click **Proofing** options and make sure **Check spelling as you type** is checked. Click **OK**. Unrecognised words will be underlined in red as soon as they are entered.*

⟳ Manoeuvres

1. Open the document **Ufo**. Add a title **UFO** in bold.

2. With the cursor at the top of the document, display the **Review** tab.

3. Click the **Spelling & Grammar** button in the **Proofing** group to check for spelling errors and deal with them appropriately.

4. The first word to be highlighted is **aproached**.

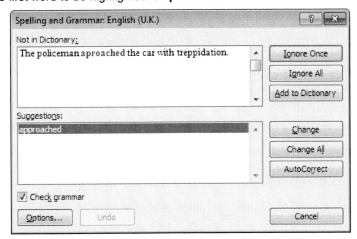

5. From the **Suggestions**, select **approached** and click on **Change** (**Change All** will change each occurrence of the word in the document).

continued over

Driving Lesson 45 - Continued

6. Continue in this way, dealing with each selected word, or grammatical error, choosing to change, ignore, delete, etc., as required. If the selected word needs to be added to the dictionary, then **Add** should be selected. Some of the errors found will be repeated words.

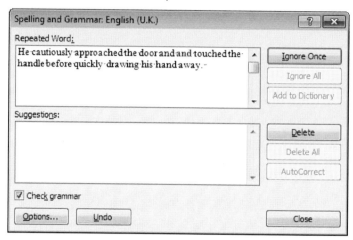

7. Click the **Delete** button in the dialog box to remove the second occurrence of the word.

> *Notice the **Spell Book** on the **Status Bar**. This indicates the current status of the document. If there are mistakes, appears; if everything is correct, appears. Double clicking on the book will display a short menu providing alternatives for a single spelling error. Right clicking an incorrectly spelled word will also produce a list of suggested alternatives.*

8. When the **Spelling and Grammar** check is complete, a message is displayed.

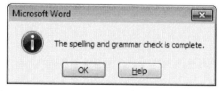

9. Click **OK**.

> *The spell checker will only highlight words that it does not have in its dictionary. It will not always detect valid words used incorrectly such as "**I like this allot**" or "**semi detached horse**". It is always advisable to proof read any important documents as a final check.*

10. Close the document <u>without</u> saving.

Driving Lesson 46 - Add to Dictionary

▣ Park and Read

Some words and proper names are not recognised automatically by *Word*. To prevent these being marked as an error each time, they can be added to the dictionary. After these words have been added, they won't appear again as errors.

⌒ Manoeuvres

1. Open the document **Maneaters**.

2. Click the **Spelling and Grammar** button. Move the dialog box by clicking and dragging its **Title Bar** if necessary to see the first error.

3. Ensure the **Check grammar** box is unchecked.

4. The first error found is displayed. Click **Ignore Once** to ignore the title of the document.

5. The next error is highlighted. **Catshark** is a proper name. Click **Add to Dictionary** to add the word to the dictionary.

ⓘ *If someone else has worked through this Driving Lesson on your computer, the word may already be in the dictionary, as it can only be added once.*

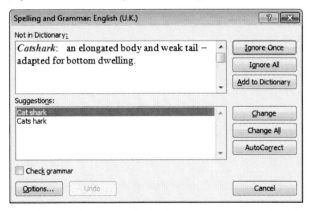

6. All the remaining words are zoological terms or names. **Add** them all to the dictionary. Click **OK** when the spelling check complete message appears and move to the end of the document.

7. To ensure the dictionary has been updated type the following words: **oophagy**, **denticles** and **swellshark**. Notice how the words are not underlined.

8. Leave the document open.

Driving Lesson 47 - Hyphenation

▣ Park and Read

Hyphens help to remove surplus space from justified text and narrow columns by splitting words on to two lines. Hyphenation can be applied to documents manually or automatically. If you choose to hyphenate automatically, *Word* decides where to place the hyphens; if you choose manual hyphenation, then you can accept or reject each hyphenation suggested.

⟱ Manoeuvres

1. Use the document **Maneaters**. This document is **justified** – it has straight left and right margins.

2. Move to the beginning of the document.

3. Click the **Page Layout** tab and in the **Page Setup** group select **Hyphenation**.

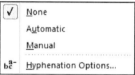

4. Select **Automatic** option.

5. Scroll through the document to see where the hyphens have been added.

6. Click **Undo** to cancel the hyphenation then select **Hyphenation** again.

7. Select **Manual** to perform the hyphenation manually. The first suggested hyphenation is displayed.

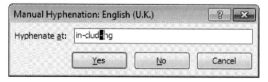

8. Click **Yes** to accept the hyphenation. Accept or reject the remaining suggestions until hyphenation is complete.

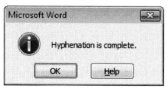

9. Click **OK**.

10. Close the document <u>without</u> saving.

Driving Lesson 48 - Searching a Document

◻ Park and Read

Visually searching for a character, word or phrase in a document can be tedious. The **Find** command moves directly to a specific word or string of characters. You can search for every occurrence of a specified word or phrase.

⌕ Manoeuvres

1.   Open the document **Golf**.

2.   With the **Home** tab displayed click the **Find** button in the **Editing** group. The **Document Navigation** pane is then displayed.

ℹ *Pressing <**Ctrl F**> will also display the **Document Navigation** pane.*

3.   Enter the word **meeting** in the **Search Document** box.

4.   Every instance of the word **meeting** is highlighted in the main view of the document and is listed in the **Document Navigation** pane.

5.   The total number of occurrences is also displayed on the **Document Navigation** pane.

6.   To search for a phrase, in the **Search Document** box delete the existing text and type **delay the appointment**. The requested phrase is found in the last paragraph.

7.   Close the **Navigation Pane** and leave the document open.

Driving Lesson 49 - Replace

▣ Park and Read

The **Replace** facility works in a similar way to **Find**; it gives the option to exchange each chosen occurrence of a character, word or phrase with an alternative.

↰ Manoeuvres

1.   Use the document **Golf**. To replace the name **Bloomfield** with **Broomfield**, place the cursor at the beginning of the document and click the **Replace** button from the **Editing** group on the **Home** tab.

ℹ️ *The **Replace** tab of the **Find and Replace** dialog box can also be displayed by pressing <**Ctrl H**>.*

2.   Enter **Bloomfield** in the **Find what** box (make sure it replaces any existing text) and **Broomfield** in **Replace with** box.

3.   Select **Find Next** to identify the first occurrence of the name then click **Replace**. Click **OK** at the end of the search.

4.   Replace the phrase **Finance and General Purposes Committee** with **Golf Club Directors'**, by entering the first phrase in the **Find what** box and the second in the **Replace with** box and then clicking **Replace All**.

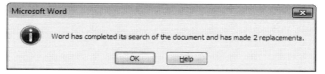

5.   Click **OK** when the message above appears and close the **Find and Replace** dialog box by clicking on **Close**.

6.   Use **Find** to check the changes. Save the document as **Golf2** and close it.

7.   Open the document **Exchange**. The exchange trip is actually between France and the US. All instances of **£** must be replaced with **$**.

8.   Click **Replace,** from the **Editing** group. In **Find what** enter **£** and in **Replace with** enter **$** (the dollar sign can be found above the number keys. Even if there is only a Euro symbol, **€**, holding down <**Shift**> while pressing the key will still create a dollar sign).

9.   Click **Replace All** and click **OK** at the completed search message. **Close** the **Find and Replace** dialog box.

10. Save the document as **American Exchange** and close it.

Driving Lesson 50 - Zoom Control

🅿 Park and Read

Zoom Control is a facility, which allows a document to be viewed in various magnifications. It will allow the document to be reduced or increased in size thus allowing more or less of a document to be displayed on screen.

☞ Manoeuvres

1. Open the document **Retail**.

2. On the **Status Bar** there is a **Zoom** slider. Notice the percentage indicator shows the current zoom level, 100% in this example.

3. Click and drag the slider slightly to the left, the magnification percentage is reduced, showing more of the page, but making it more difficult to read.

4. Use the ⊞ on the slider to increase the zoom level to **120%**.

5. Display the **View** tab. The **Zoom** group contains buttons that control how the document is displayed.

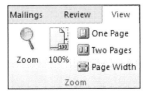

6. Click to **100%** button to return the view to normal.

7. Click the **One Page** button to display a full page on screen.

8. Click the **Two Pages** button to display two pages side by side.

9. Click the **Page Width** button to display a page across the width of the screen.

10. Click the **Zoom** button, this displays **Zoom** dialog box. Select the **Many pages** option. Click the drop down on the screen below **Many pages**. Select **1 x 3 Pages** by clicking and dragging on the diagram. This will display three pages side by side on screen at the same time.

11. Click **OK** to apply the view to the document.

12. Change the view of the document back to **100%** using any method.

13. Close the document <u>without</u> saving.

Driving Lesson 51 - Preferences

▣ Park and Read

Basic options (**preferences**) can be set in *Word*, for example the user name, which is automatically added to certain templates. By default documents are opened from and saved to the **Documents** folder. These default locations can also be changed.

⟰ Manoeuvres

1. Close *Word* and then start *Word* again. This is so the default settings can be seen. Click the **File** tab and select **Open** and notice that the **Open** dialog box shows **Documents library** as the default location.

ℹ️ *As you have been opening files from the **3 Word Processing** folder, this would have been the default folder if the program had not been closed in step 1.*

2. Click **Cancel** to close the dialog box and click 🖫 on the **Quick Access Toolbar**. The **Save As** dialog box also saves by default to the **Documents library**. Click **Cancel**.

3. To change this file location, click the **File** tab and then the **Options** button. In the **Word Options** window, display the **Save** section.

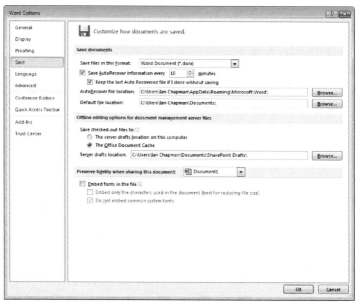

4. To change the **Default file location**, click **Browse** to the right of the box.

continued over

Driving Lesson 51 - Continued

5.   To open and save using the **Desktop**, expand **Favorites** from the navigation pane and select **Desktop**. Click **OK**.

 *Any folder could have been selected in the **Modify Location** dialog box.*

6.   Click **OK** again.

7.   Click the **File** tab and click **Open**. Notice now that the **Desktop** is the default location.

8.   Click **Cancel**. Check the **Save As** dialog box to see where the document would be saved to.

9.   **Cancel** the dialog box.

10. To change the file locations back to **Documents**, click the **File** tab and then **Options**. Click **Save** and then **Browse** next to the **Default file location** box.

11. Expand **Libraries**, if necessary and select the **Documents** folder then click **OK**.

12. Select **General**.

13. To change the user details enter your own name in **User name** and your initials in **Initials**, under **Personalize your copy of Microsoft Office**.

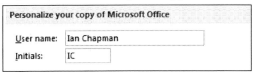

14. Click **OK** to accept the changes.

15. Close any open documents.

Driving Lesson 52 - Revision

This covers the features introduced in this section. Try not to refer to the preceding Driving Lessons while completing it.

1. Open the document **Mistooks**, from the **3 Word Processing** data folder. How many possible spelling errors are identified?

2. Ensure that the cursor is at the beginning of the document and start the **Spelling and Grammar Checker**.

3. Use the **Spelling and Grammar Checker** to correct any spelling mistakes.

4. Use the **Replace** facility to change the word **cheering** to the word **pleasant**.

5. Using **Replace**, change **lottery** to **Lotto**.

6. Ensure that the cursor is at the beginning of the document.

7. Use the **Find** facility to find the first occurrence of the word **probability** within the document.

8. How many times matches are found?

9. Close the document <u>without</u> saving changes.

10. Open the document **Phone** and then change the **Zoom** to **150%**.

11. Underline the title, then change the **Zoom** to **100%**.

12. Read the document through. How many words have jagged red lines below them?

13. Check the document for spelling. Correct the errors found.

14. The spelling checker does not find the irregular case of **DO** at the start of the last sentence or **contract** which should be **contact**. Make these changes manually.

15. Obtain a printed copy of **Phone**, and close it <u>without</u> saving.

16. Open the document **Kingtut**.

17. Apply automatic hyphenation to the document.

18. Print the document.

19. Close it <u>without</u> saving.

 *Answers are shown in the **Answers** section at the end of this guide.*

If you experienced any difficulty completing the Revision, refer back to the Driving Lessons in this section. Then redo the Revision.

Driving Lesson 53 - Revision

This covers the features introduced in this section. Try not to refer to the preceding Driving Lessons while completing it.

1. Open the document **Cat**.

2. Apply automatic hyphenation to the document.

3. Replace all occurrences of the name **Wanda** with **Wilma**.

4. Replace all occurrences of the name **Pyewacket** with **Grimalkin**.

5. Add your name to the end of the text.

6. Print a single copy of the document.

7. Close the document <u>without</u> saving.

8. Start a new document.

9. Change the location from which files are opened by default to the **3 Word Processing** folder (see page 4 **Downloading the Data Files** for the location).

10. Check that the preferences have been changed by closing and then reopening *Word*, then using **Open** to view the default location.

11. Change the default open location back to **Documents**.

12. Close any open documents <u>without</u> saving.

If you experienced any difficulty completing the Revision, refer back to the Driving Lessons in this section. Then redo the Revision.

Once you are confident with the features, complete the Record of Achievement Matrix referring to the section at the end of the guide. Only when competent move on to the next Section.

Section 7
Formatting Paragraphs

By the end of this Section you should be able to:

Align Text

Indent Paragraphs

Apply Advanced Indentation

Apply Bullets and Numbers

Change Line and Paragraph Spacing

Apply and Change Tab Settings

Change Tab Alignment

Apply Borders and Shading

To gain an understanding of the above features, work through the **Driving Lessons** in this **Section**.

For each **Driving Lesson**, read the **Park and Read** instructions, without touching the keyboard, then work through the numbered steps of the **Manoeuvres** on the computer. Complete the **Revision Exercise(s)** at the end of the section to test your knowledge.

Driving Lesson 54 - Alignment

▣ Park and Read

Alignment refers to where text appears on each line in relation to the margins. *Word* is capable of four types of text alignment: **Left** - straight left margin, uneven right margin, **Centred** - aligned with the centre of the page, **Right** - uneven left margin, straight right margin and **Justified** - straight left and right margins. It's often a matter of preference which alignment you use, but justified text looks much neater. Rather than adding spaces, aligning text using the **Alignment** buttons such as; **Center**, **Align Text Right** and **Justify**, is good practice for achieving consistent results.

↱ Manoeuvres

1. Open the document **Cia**.

2. Embolden **quality** in the first paragraph and the names of the founders in the same paragraph.

3. Alignment selection is made by selecting the alignment buttons which are found in the **Paragraph** group on the **Home** tab.

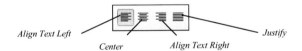

Align Text Left   Center   Align Text Right   Justify

4. Highlight the first paragraph. Click the **Justify** button, ▤. Note that the text now has straight right and left margins.

5. If only one paragraph is to be aligned, the insertion point needs only to be placed in the paragraph, for the effect to take place. Position the cursor within the second paragraph. Right align the text by clicking the **Align Text Right** button, ▤.

6. Click in the third paragraph and click the **Center** button, ▤. The text is aligned about the centre of each line.

7. With the cursor in the same paragraph, click the **Align Text Left** button, ▤. The text returns to its default, left alignment.

8. Print out a copy of the text.

9. Close the document <u>without</u> saving any changes.

Driving Lesson 55 - Indenting Paragraphs

▣ Park and Read

An indented paragraph is one where the left edge of the text is further from the margin than the other paragraphs. It is possible to indent the first line of a paragraph by a different amount to the rest of the paragraph (see next Driving Lesson). The <**Tab**> key is used to indent just the first line of a paragraph, but the **Increase Indent** button, ⊞, from the **Paragraph** group is used to indent a whole paragraph a set amount (1.27 cm). Each time the button is pressed, the paragraph is indented to the next tab stop. Indents can also be controlled using different amounts by using the **Paragraph** dialog box. As good practice, indents (or the <**Tab**> key) should be used to indent paragraphs properly - do not use the spacebar to add spaces and align text.

⌒ Manoeuvres

1. Open the document **Warehouse**.

2. Fully justify the second paragraph.

3. Indent the third and fourth paragraphs to the first tab stop by selecting them and using the **Increase Indent** button, ⊞.

ⓘ *Click the **Increase Indent** or **Decrease Indent** buttons as many times as necessary to indent the paragraphs by the required amount.*

4. Place the insertion point in the third paragraph and click the **Decrease Indent** button, ⊞, to remove the indentation.

ⓘ *There are key presses for these functions, Increase Indent <**Ctrl M**>. Decrease Indent <**Ctrl Shift M**>.*

5. Indent the fifth paragraph to the second tab stop by selecting it and clicking the **Increase Indent** button twice.

6. Place the cursor in the sixth paragraph and click the **Paragraph** dialog box launcher. Indents can be controlled to exactly using boxes under **Left** and **Right**. Use the spinner to increase the **Left** indent to **2 cm**.

7. Click **OK**. The paragraph is indented to 2 cm.

8. Print preview the document to observe the effect of using indents.

9. Close the document <u>without</u> saving the changes that have been made.

Driving Lesson 56 - Advanced Indentation

🅿 Park and Read

Right, **Left** and **First Line** indent markers are displayed on the ruler. These enable you to produce customised indents, without the need for re-setting the tabs.

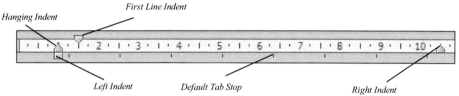

Hanging Indent

First Line Indent

Left Indent   *Default Tab Stop*   *Right Indent*

👣 Manoeuvres

1. Open **Warehouse** again and make sure the ruler is visible. If it is not, display the **View** tab and check **Ruler** in the **Show** group.

2. Position the cursor in the third paragraph.

3. Click and drag the left indent marker (square) on the left of the ruler, to **1cm** on the ruler.

4. When the mouse button is released, all lines of the paragraph will be indented to that position.

5. Click and drag the first line indent marker (top triangle) on the left of the ruler, to **2cm** on the ruler.

6. When the mouse button is released the first line of the paragraph will be indented to that position.

7. Still in the same paragraph, indent the right side of the paragraph by selecting and dragging the triangle at the bottom right of the ruler to **13cm**. When the mouse button is released the paragraph will be indented from the right.

ℹ️ *By dragging the hanging indent marker (lower triangle) to a position on the ruler, the whole paragraph will be indented, except the first line which will remain the same. Hanging indents are not part of this syllabus.*

8. Justify the paragraph. Now spend a few minutes experimenting.

9. Close **Warehouse** <u>without</u> saving.

Driving Lesson 57 - Bullets and Numbering

ⓟ Park and Read

Word has the ability to automatically number lists and paragraphs. In each case, a hanging indent will also be applied. This separates the text from the numbering and improves the appearance of the document. Different styles of numbering and bullets can be applied to text, using the drop downs on the buttons.

⌒ Manoeuvres

1. Open the document **Warehouse** again.

2. Select the six paragraphs of text and number them by clicking on the **Numbering** button, ⊞, from the **Paragraph** group.

3. Save the numbered document as **numbers** and **preview** it.

4. Return to normal view by selecting the **Home** tab. Position the cursor within the second paragraph. Click the **Numbering** button, ⊞, to remove the number. Notice how *Word* has automatically renumbered the other paragraphs.

5. Remove all of the paragraph numbering by selecting the numbered paragraphs and clicking the **Numbering** button, ⊞.

6. Select all the paragraphs and click the **Bullets** button, ⊞.

7. Select the second and third paragraphs. Click the **Bullets** button again to remove the bullets.

8. Remove all bullets from the paragraphs and close the document, <u>without</u> saving the changes.

9. Open the document **Books** and select the list, but not the headings.

10. Click the drop down arrow on the **Numbering** button to display the **Numbering Library** options, shown overleaf.

continued over

Driving Lesson 57 - Continued

The list may not look exactly like the one above, but a form of roman numerals should be available.

11. Move the cursor over the **Numbering Library** options to see the list on the page change. Finally click on the lower case roman numerals (i, ii, etc.).

12. With all items still selected, display the **Numbering Library** options again and select **Define New Number Format**.

13. Click the **Number Style** drop down and select **A, B, C**. Now click the **Font** button and select **Verdana** (or an alternative). Click **OK**, then **OK** again to apply the customised numbering.

14. With all items still selected, display the **Numbering Library** options again and select **Set Numbering Value**.

15. Amend the **Set value to C** using the spinner and click **OK**. The numbering sequence now starts from **C**.

16. Select all of the numbered items, then click the **Bullets** drop down arrow. Select the **check tick**, (or another bullet style if this one is not available).

17. Select the **Bullets** drop down again and select **Define New Bullet**.

18. Click the **Picture** button. Select an alternative symbol for the bullet and click **OK**, then **OK** again.

19. Save the document as **bulleted** and close it.

Driving Lesson 58 - Line Spacing

▣ Park and Read

Line spacing offers a simple way of improving the appearance and readability of a document. The default setting for line spacing in *Word 2010* is **1.15** lines. Other useful line spacing settings are **Double** and **1½**. However, this may not be suitable if creating a list, a table, or if a feature such as superscript is used.

⌐ Manoeuvres

1. Open the document **Camera**. Remove the top line and add your own name to the bottom of the document.

2. Select all the text, then click the **Justify** button.

3. The **Line Spacing** has been set to **Single**, i.e. **1.0**, for this document. The default Line Spacing for *Word 2010* documents is **1.15**. Place the cursor in the second paragraph and click the **Line Spacing** button [⭦≡⭥▾].

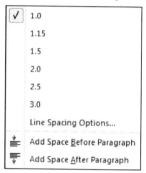

4. Select **1.5** from the drop down list to change the **Line spacing** to one and half for the second paragraph.

5. Place the cursor in the third paragraph, click the **Line Spacing** button and select **2.0** to change the **Line spacing** to double.

6. Use the **Print Preview** facility to check the appearance of the text.

ⓘ *To quickly apply line spacing, position the cursor within a paragraph. Press <Ctrl 1> for single spacing. Press <Ctrl 5> for one and a half spacing. Press <Ctrl 2> for double spacing.*

7. Save the document as **cam2**.

8. Practice changing the line spacing for the paragraphs by using the quick presses for single, one and half and double.

9. Close the document <u>without</u> saving.

Driving Lesson 59 - Spacing Between Paragraphs

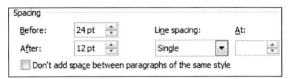 Park and Read

Spacing between paragraphs can also be adjusted. Spacing is measured in **pt**. **12pt** is 1 line for a size 12 font. It's good practice to use proper paragraph spacing rather than the **<Return>** key; do it this way to make sure paragraph spacing is consistent. The default paragraph spacing for *Word 2010* is 10pt after the paragraph.

Manoeuvres

1.   Open the document **Warehouse**.

2.   Remove the blank lines between the paragraphs.

3.   Select the entire document and click the **Line spacing** button.

4.   Select **Add Space Before Paragraph**. This adds by default a **12pt** space before each paragraph.

5.   To control exactly how much space is added, click the **Line spacing** button and then **Line Spacing Options**.

6.   Under **Spacing**, increase the **Before** option to **24** pt.

7.   To leave spacing after the paragraphs, increase the **After** option to **12** pt.

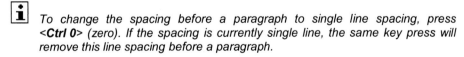

8.   Click **OK** (it is not a normal practice to increase both **Before** and **After** for the same paragraphs).

[i] *To change the spacing before a paragraph to single line spacing, press* **<Ctrl 0>** *(zero). If the spacing is currently single line, the same key press will remove this line spacing before a paragraph.*

9.   **Preview** the document.

10.   Close the document without saving.

Driving Lesson 60 - Tab Settings

Park and Read

Tabs are a precise measurement for aligning vertical rows of text in a document. Tabs are set by default every 1.27cm. Tabs, rather than spaces, should be used to align text properly. New tab settings will only apply to text that has been selected, or is yet to be typed. Left alignment **Tab** settings are displayed as **L**'s on the ruler.

Manoeuvres

1.   Start a new document. The ruler should be displayed, if not check **Ruler** in the **Show/Hide** group on the **View** tab.

2.   Click the **Paragraph** dialog box launcher, on the **Home** tab.

Dialog Box Launcher

3.   The **Paragraph** dialog box is displayed. Click the **Tabs** button.

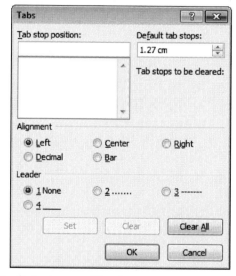

4.   Enter **1** cm in the **Tab stop position** box.

5.   Check the **Alignment** is **Left** and the **Leader** is **None**.

6.   Click **Set** and then click **OK**. An **L** appears on the **Ruler** at **1cm**.

7.   A quicker, easier way to set **Tabs**, is to click the required position on the ruler. Click at **10** on the ruler, an **L** will appear when it is set.

continued over

Driving Lesson 60 - Continued

8. **Tab Positions** can be changed by clicking on the **L** and dragging along the ruler to the required position. Change the **10cm** tab stop to **5cm** by dragging.

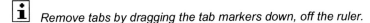 *Remove tabs by dragging the tab markers down, off the ruler.*

9. Type in the following text, using the <**Tab**> key before each piece of text to move to the next tab stop and the <**Enter**> key to start a new line. Start each new line with a <**Tab**>.

Salesperson	Sales
J Heslop	126.56
M Patel	56
K Lowe	340.75
D Green	9.5
S Evans	1200
A Hargreaves	50.98

10. Save the text as **tabs**.

11. Select the entire document and clear the tab settings, by dragging the tab stops off the ruler.

12. With the entire document selected use the mouse and ruler to set tabs at approximately **2cm** and **7cm**.

13. Close the document <u>without</u> saving the changes.

14. Open the document **Contents**.

15. Select the whole document then click the left tab marker and drag to about **5cm**. Release the mouse button. The first column will move.

16. Click the second tab marker and drag it to **11cm**.

17. Drag the **5cm** tab stop down off the ruler. The text automatically shifts to the next tab marker.

18. Create a new tab stop at **3cm**.

19. Practice using the mouse and ruler to move and remove tab markers.

20. Close the document **Contents** <u>without</u> saving.

Driving Lesson 61 - Tab Alignment

P Park and Read

Word has five types of tab settings. The important four are **Left**, **Centre**, **Right** and **Decimal**. Each of these determines how text is aligned at a particular tab stop position.

Manoeuvres

1.　Re-open the document **Contents**.

2.　Select the whole document and use the ruler to move the tab positions to **4cm** and **11cm**.

3.　Point at the **4cm** tab position and double click. This displays the **Tabs** dialog box. Notice it is left aligned.

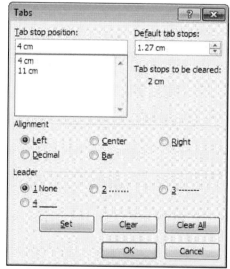

4.　Select the **Right** option from the **Alignment** selections. Click **Set**.

5.　Select the **11cm** tab from the **Tab stop position** box, and make it **Center** aligned. Click **Set**.

6.　Click **OK** and observe the text positioning about the tabs.

i *Tabs can be set directly from the ruler by clicking* ⌊L⌋ *on the left end of the* ***Ruler*** *bar. The tabs alternate between* ⌊L⌋, ⌊⊥⌋, ⌊◢⌋, ⌊⊥⌋, ⌊I⌋, ⌊▽⌋ *and* ⌊▭⌋ *(Left, Centre, Right, Decimal, Bar, First Line Indent, Hanging Indent). Click the ruler to place a tab stop of the current type at the position required.*

continued over

Driving Lesson 61 - Continued

7.   Select the whole document again and experiment by changing the tabs into right, left and centre tabs. Close the document <u>without</u> saving.

8.   Create a new document. Set the **Font Size** to **10pt** and enter the following text, pressing **<Tab>** between each piece of text to move it to the next available tab stop. Click **Show/Hide**, 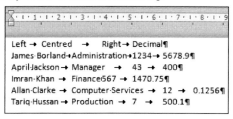, to view the tab control characters (arrows pointing right). These are special, non-printing characters used by *Word* to control formatting.

```
Left → Centred    →    Right→ Decimal¶
James·Borland→Administration→1234→ 5678.9¶
April·Jackson→ Manager    →    43  →  400¶
Imran·Khan  →  Finance567 → 1470.75¶
Allan·Clarke → Computer·Services  →  12  →  0.1256¶
Tariq·Hussan→ Production  →  7   →   500.1¶
```

ℹ️ *Some tab controls may not be displayed where there is not enough space between the words. This does not matter.*

9.   Select the whole document and change the current tab setting by clicking once on the ⌐ at the left end of the ruler to change it to a **Centre** tab, ⊥. Then place a centre tab at **4**cm by clicking on the number **4** on the ruler.

10. Click once on ⊥ to change it to a **Right** tab, ⌐ and place a right tab at **8**cm by clicking on **8** on the ruler.

11. Click once on ⌐ to change it to a **Decimal** tab, ⊥ and place a decimal tab at **10**cm by clicking on **10** on the ruler.

12. Click **Show/Hide** ¶ to hide the tab control characters. Examine the effects of the different types of tab alignment.

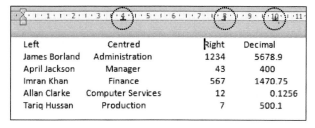

Left	Centred	Right	Decimal
James Borland	Administration	1234	5678.9
April Jackson	Manager	43	400
Imran Khan	Finance	567	1470.75
Allan Clarke	Computer Services	12	0.1256
Tariq Hussan	Production	7	500.1

13. Close the document <u>without</u> saving.

ℹ️ *To change the type of a tab stop, you need to **remove** the **existing** one by dragging it off the ruler, before **replacing** it with one of the required type.*

Driving Lesson 62 - Adding Borders

Park and Read

Borders can be created around text or whole pages. The options are: **None** - removes borders, **Box** - same border around the whole object, **Shadow** - a drop shadow around the text. **3-D** - offsets and highlights the border, while **Custom** allows borders to be applied around any side independent of the other sides. Shading can also be added to specific paragraphs for emphasis.

Manoeuvres

1. Open **Letter1**. Select all the text and ensure the **Home** tab is displayed.

2. In the **Paragraph** group click the **Borders** drop down and select **Borders and Shading**.

The button's appearance will show an icon representing its previous setting.

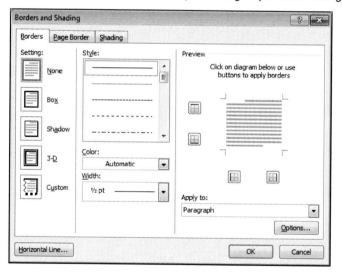

3. From the **Borders** tab select **Box**. From the **Style** options select any dashed line and then click on **OK**. A dashed line border should now surround the text of the document.

4. To remove the border, click the **Borders** drop down menu and select **No Border**.

5. With the whole document selected, click the **Borders** drop down and select **Borders and Shading**.

continued over

Driving Lesson 62 - Continued

6. Click **Custom** and then click the top and bottom of the **Preview** diagram at the right of the dialog box.

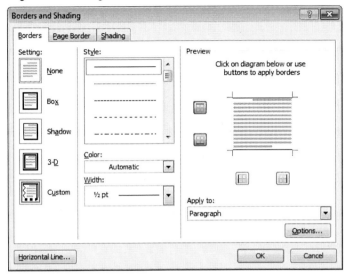

7. Click **OK**. This applies a border to the top and bottom of the text only.

ℹ️ *The appearance of the border can be changed by applying different settings for.* ***Style, Color*** *and* ***Width.***

8. Display the **Borders and Shading** dialog box and select the **Page Border** tab. The options here are exactly the same as before but the settings will apply to the whole page, regardless of content.

9. Select a **Box** border with a double line style, line width **1½ pt** and red colour. Click **OK**. Notice the difference between this **Page Border** around the whole page and the previous border which applies to the text only.

10. Close the document <u>without</u> saving.

11. Open the document **Maneaters**.

12. To make the **Conclusion** stand out, it can be shaded. Click anywhere in the paragraph immediately under the **Conclusion** heading.

13. Select **Borders and Shading** from the **Borders** drop down and display the **Shading** tab.

14. Choose a light shade of grey from the **Fill** drop down box. Click **OK** to apply the shading.

15. Close the document <u>without</u> saving.

Driving Lesson 63 - Revision

This covers the features introduced in this section. Try not to refer to the preceding Driving Lessons while completing it.

1. Open the document **Canyon**.

2. Insert the title **The Grand Canyon** on its own line at the start of the document and align it centrally.

3. Leave a blank line after the title.

4. Justify the first paragraph.

5. Right align the second paragraph.

6. Centre the third paragraph.

7. Select the final paragraph, it is already left aligned, click the **Align Text Left** button and it removes left alignment and justifies the paragraph.

8. Apply left alignment using the button again.

9. Print a copy of the document in its current form.

10. Close the document <u>without</u> saving any changes.

11. Open the document **Questions**.

12. This contains 14 statements. Use a button to number them.

13. Use the **Print Preview** facility to check the results.

14. Alter the **First Line Indent** on the ruler to **2.5**cm.

15. Remove all numbering (the indent is changed).

16. Bullet this list using the button.

17. Print preview the document.

18. Save a copy of the document as **Questions2**.

19. Close the document.

If you experienced any difficulty completing the Revision, refer back to the Driving Lessons in this section. Then redo the Revision.

Driving Lesson 64 - Revision

This covers the features introduced in this section. Try not to refer to the preceding Driving Lessons while completing it.

1.   Open the document **Banking**.

2.   Increase the size of the text to **18pt** and print the document.

3.   Right align the first paragraph and apply a border to it.

4.   Use justified alignment for the second paragraph.

5.   Print a copy of the document, then close it <u>without</u> saving.

6.   A printed menu must be produced for lunch. Open a new document and create a three course lunch of your choice with a small selection for each course. Separate each course with a row of suitably spaced £ signs.

7.   Add a suitable title in bold and underline.

8.   Centrally align the menu and adjust the line spacing.

9.   Print a copy of your menu, save the document as **Lunch** then close it.

10. Open the document **Books** and select all the text except for the title.

11. Apply **Numbering** to the selected lines of text.

12. The number indent is interfering with the first tab maker. Remove the first tab marker from the ruler, so that the text is correctly aligned.

13. Print a copy of the document.

14. Remove the **Numbering** from the lines of text and replace with **Bullets**.

15. Customise the **Bullets** by choosing alternative symbols.

16. Print preview the document, then close it <u>without</u> saving any changes.

17. Open **Diary**. This is a tabbed document with all the tabs set as left tabs.

18. Change the settings for the **Time** and **Activity** columns as follows:

     Change the **Time** tab at **6.5cm** to a **Center** tab.

     Change the **Activity** tab at **11.25cm** to a **Right** tab.

19. Change the font of the headings to **Comic Sans MS**.

20. Print preview the document and print it, then close the document <u>without</u> saving the changes.

If you experienced any difficulty completing the Revision, refer back to the Driving Lessons in this section. Then redo the Revision.

Once you are confident with the features, complete the Record of Achievement Matrix referring to the section at the end of the guide. Only when competent move on to the next Section.

Section 8
Multiple Documents

By the end of this Section you should be able to:

Switch between open Documents

Cut, Copy and Paste between Documents

Apply Headers and Footers

Apply Page Numbering

To gain an understanding of the above features, work through the **Driving Lessons** in this **Section**.

For each **Driving Lesson**, read the **Park and Read** instructions, without touching the keyboard, then work through the numbered steps of the **Manoeuvres** on the computer. Complete the **Revision Exercise(s)** at the end of the section to test your knowledge.

Driving Lesson 65 - Switch Between Documents

▣ Park and Read

Many documents can be open at the same time using *Word*. A button on the **Taskbar** lists the documents that are open, making it easier to switch between them. To see the documents that are open, place the mouse over the **Word** button on the **Taskbar** and a list of documents is displayed. The document that is being currently worked on is known as the **active document** and is distinguished from the others by being shaded on the list. If more than one document can be seen on screen, the active document is said to be present in the **active window** and is indicated by darker coloured writing on the **Title Bar**.

Opening a second document places it on screen in a new window, the document previously active can still be accessed by using the **Word** button.

⌒ Manoeuvres

1. Open the document **Retail** and type your name at the start of the document so that it can be readily identified.

2. Open the document **Camera**. Both documents are now open.

3. Move the mouse over the **Word** button on the **Taskbar**, . A list of open documents is displayed. Click **Retail** from the list to display that window.

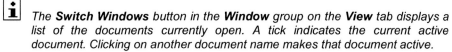

4. Open the document **Cia**. Practice switching between active documents using the **Taskbar**.

ℹ️ *The **Switch Windows** button in the **Window** group on the **View** tab displays a list of the documents currently open. A tick indicates the current active document. Clicking on another document name makes that document active.*

5. From the **View** tab, click the **Arrange All** button from the **Window** group. All the opened documents will be shown on screen. Click on the window of **Camera** to make it active.

6. Click on the **Retail** window. The size of the window for **Camera** does not change, although it may be overlapped.

7. Maximise **Retail** by clicking on the **Maximize** button, ▭.

8. Close the document **Retail**. Do not save any changes made to the document.

9. Close all the remaining documents (the last document may have to be maximised to show the **Ribbon** and **File** tab), leaving *Word* open.

Driving Lesson 66 - Cut, Copy, Paste Between Documents

▣ Park and Read

It is a relatively simple process to cut or copy text from one document and paste it into a new document, or elsewhere in the existing document. A **Smart Tag** will appear after pasting to allow **Paste Options** to be selected.

↱ Manoeuvres

1. Open the document **Parts** and select the entire document.

2. Change the font of all text to **Arial 11pt**.

3. Open the document **Planning**.

4. Select the title **Production Planning** and its associated paragraph.

5. Click the **Cut** button, 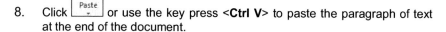, in the **Clipboard** group on the **Home** tab (or use the key press <**Ctrl X**>).

6. Use the *Word* button on the **Taskbar** to switch to the **Parts** document.

7. Position the cursor at the end of the document.

8. Click 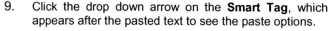 or use the key press <**Ctrl V**> to paste the paragraph of text at the end of the document.

9. Click the drop down arrow on the **Smart Tag**, which appears after the pasted text to see the paste options.

10. Click **Merge Formatting,** the second icon, to convert the pasted text to the same format as the existing text.

11. Press <**Enter**> to separate the paragraphs as required.

12. Switch back to **Planning**.

13. Select paragraph number 7, complete with its title. Use the **Copy** button, 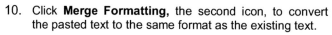 and then the **Paste** button to copy this to the end of the **Parts** document.

14. Adjust the spacing and formatting as necessary.

15. Try moving and/or copying text from the **Parts** document to **Planning**.

16. Close both the documents <u>without</u> saving.

Driving Lesson 67 - Headers and Footers

▣ Park and Read

Headers and **Footers** are common identification lines at the top and/or bottom of each printed page. You can type into a header or footer, so that it will appear on every page in the document. When such text is found at the top of a page it is called a **Header**; those at the bottom are termed **Footers**. Headers and Footers can be placed on alternate pages, or the same header/footer on every page.

☞ Manoeuvres

1.   Open the document **Retail**. Delete the title line.

2.   Display the **Insert** tab and click **Header** button in the **Header and Footer** group.

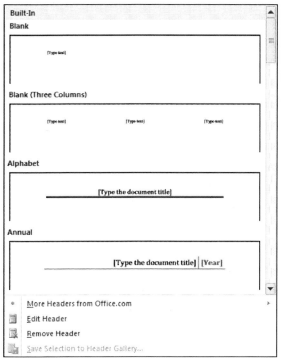

3.   Select the **Alphabet** style. The default title was the first line of the original text - **COMPUTERS AND RETAILING**.

4.   To replace the text, click **Title** and type a new one. Enter **Computers In Retailing by I. Knowitall**.

continued over

Driving Lesson 67 - Continued

5. Select this text, change the font colour to red and the font to **Tahoma**.

6. Creating a **Header** adds the **Header & Footer Tools Design** tab to the **Ribbon**. Make sure this tab is displayed then click the **Go to Footer** button.

7. Special features such as the date, time and page numbering can be added by selecting the correct button from the **Ribbon**.

8. Click the **Footer** button from the **Ribbon** and select **Blank (Three Columns)**.

9. Type your name in the left column, add a space then click the **Date & Time** button on the Ribbon. From the **Date and Time** dialog box, select the second option that displays the day and date format. Click **OK**.

10. Place the cursor in the centre column and click the **Page Number** button from the **Ribbon**. From the list select **Current Position**, then **Plain Number** style from the list.

11. To insert the name of the file, place the cursor in the right column and click the **Quick Parts** button. Click **Field** and select **FileName** from the list and **First capital** from the **Format** list. Click **OK**.

12. Click the **Close Header and Footer** button.

13. Check the appearance of the headers and footers by previewing the document. Scroll through the document to see them on every page.

ℹ️ *The **Headers** are removed by clicking the **Header** button and selecting **Remove Header**. **Footers** are removed in a similar way but with **Footer** and **Remove Footer**.*

ℹ️ *When using any 3 column header or footer, any unused **[Type text]** areas must be deleted or they will be printed.*

14. Close the document <u>without</u> saving.

Driving Lesson 68 - Page Numbering

▣ Park and Read

Page Numbering is added to documents using the **Page Number** button as shown in the last lesson, as part of a **footer**. Various formats can be applied to page numbers.

↱ Manoeuvres

1.   Open the document **Pc**.

2.   Display the **Insert** tab and click the **Page Number** button in the **Header & Footer** group. Select **Bottom of Page** and **Plain Number 1**.

3.   The **Design** tab for **Header & Footer Tools** is displayed. Click **Page Number** in the **Header & Footer** group and select **Format Page Numbers** from the list.

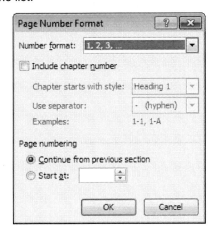

4.   From **Number format**, select **Upper Case Roman** (I, II, III…).

5.   Other options are controlled by using the **Page numbering** section. The numbering can be started at any value. Select **Start at** and enter or change the value to **II**. Click **OK**. The pages are numbered starting with two in Roman numerals.

6.   Close the document <u>without</u> saving.

ⓘ *Page numbers are removed by clicking the **Page Number** button and selecting* ***Remove Page Numbers***.

Driving Lesson 69 - Revision

This covers the features introduced in this section. Try not to refer to the preceding Driving Lessons while completing it.

1. Open the document **Canyon**.

2. Centre the title and the paragraph sub headings.

3. Justify each paragraph.

4. The final paragraph, starting with **Kaibab limestone** is to be made into a list. Remove all of the commas and the word 'and' from this paragraph.

5. After each type of rock, press <**Enter**> to create a list.

6. Add numbering to the list.

7. Add a blank **Header** to the document and add your name to it.

8. Add the date to the **Footer** using the **Date and Time** button in the **Insert** group of the **Header & Footer Tools Design** tab.

9. Print preview the document.

10. Close the document <u>without</u> saving the changes.

11. Open the documents **Pc** and **Warehouse**.

12. Copy paragraph **5** from **Warehouse – The computer may also...**

13. Switch to the document **Pc**.

14. Paste this text at the end of the **Stock Control** section on page **4**.

15. Adjust the spacing and formatting as required.

16. Add a blank **Header** to the document.

17. Insert the current date in the centre of the header.

18. Enter your name at the left of the footer.

19. Add page numbers to the right side of the footer, using the style **Accent Bar 2**.

20. Save the document as **multiples** and close it.

21. Close **Warehouse**.

If you experienced any difficulty completing the Revision, refer back to the Driving Lessons in this section. Then redo the Revision.

Driving Lesson 70 - Revision

This covers the features introduced in this section. Try not to refer to the preceding Driving Lessons while completing it.

1.   Open the document **News**.

2.   The news articles are to be arranged alphabetically by title. Use the **Cut** and **Paste** buttons to rearrange the articles. Adjust the spacing, if necessary.

3.   Add your name to the **Footer**.

4.   Print one copy of the document.

5.   Close the document <u>without</u> saving any changes.

6.   Open the document **Menu**.

7.   Centre the whole document.

8.   Increase the size of the restaurant's name, **Chez Pascale**, to **26pt**; change the font to **Lucida Handwriting**.

9.   Make it **green**.

10. Increase **Menu** to **22pt**; change the font to **Monotype Corsiva** (use an alternative font if this one is not available) and the colour to **blue**.

11. Change the size of **Entrées**, **Main Meals** and **Desserts** to **18pt** and their colour to **red**.

12. Increase the size of the meals on the menu to **14pt** and make them **blue**.

13. Add your name to the header and preview the document.

14. Close the document <u>without</u> saving.

If you experienced any difficulty completing the Revision, refer back to the Driving Lessons in this section. Then redo the Revision.

Once you are confident with the features, complete the Record of Achievement Matrix referring to the section at the end of the guide. Only when competent move on to the next Section.

Section 9
Tables

By the end of this Section you should be able to:

Insert Tables

Enter Text into Tables

Select Cells

Change Column Width/Row Height

Insert and Delete Cells

Insert and Delete Rows and Columns

Apply Borders and Shading

To gain an understanding of the above features, work through the **Driving Lessons** in this **Section**.

For each **Driving Lesson**, read the **Park and Read** instructions, without touching the keyboard, then work through the numbered steps of the **Manoeuvres** on the computer. Complete the **Revision Exercise(s)** at the end of the section to test your knowledge.

Driving Lesson 71 - Tables

▣ Park and Read

Word provides an easy way to create and edit organised rows and columns of tabular data (without tabs) using **Tables**. This feature is also useful for creating forms such as invoices that need to have a tabular format. Tables consist of rows, from top to bottom and columns, which run from left to right, to create cells as in spreadsheets.

⌦ Manoeuvres

1. Create a new document. To create a table with **4** rows and **4** columns, move the cursor to where the table is to begin. Click the **Table** button on the **Insert** tab and then select **Insert Table**.

2. In the **Insert Table** dialog box, enter **4** in the **Number of columns** box and **4** in the **Number of rows** box (these numbers can be typed in or the arrowheads can be clicked to change the numbers).

3. Click **OK** to create the table, ready for the data to be entered. Note that **Table Tools** is now a Ribbon option, with **Design** and **Layout** tabs.

4. Leave the document open for the next Driving Lesson.

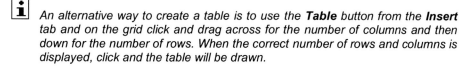

ℹ️ *An alternative way to create a table is to use the **Table** button from the **Insert** tab and on the grid click and drag across for the number of columns and then down for the number of rows. When the correct number of rows and columns is displayed, click and the table will be drawn.*

Driving Lesson 72 - Entering Text

▣ Park and Read

Once a table has been created, it is easy to enter text and move around within it. Text is edited using the normal methods. It is probably easier to type the text into the table first and then return to format the table later, i.e. correct column widths, etc.

↱ Manoeuvres

1.   Use the table created in the previous Driving Lesson. Movement forwards within a table is with **<Tab>**. Use **<Shift Tab>** to move backwards (clicking in the appropriate cell will also place the cursor). When entering text do not use **<Enter>**, unless a new line is required within the same cell, e.g. as in an address.

ℹ️ *The cursor keys can be used, but are slow when a table is full of text.*

2.   Move to the first cell and enter the following text into the table. Pay no attention to how the table looks, it will be improved later.

Company	Share Price	Sector	Type of Business
Global	1240	Chemicals	Petro Chemicals
Biro Bank	300	Banking	Corporate Finance
Gibsons	130	Stores	Electrical Retailer

ℹ️ *As text is entered, the **Move**,⊞ and **Adjust**, ▢, cursors appear top left and bottom right of the table in **Print Layout** view. **Move** is clicked and dragged to move the table around the page and **Adjust** is clicked and dragged to proportionately increase or decrease the size of the table.*

3.   The share price for **Gibsons** has risen by 50 points. To edit the table, double click on the **130** price.

4.   The number is highlighted. Type in **180** to replace the original number.

5.   Save the document as **table** and close it.

Driving Lesson 73 - Selecting Cells

▣ Park and Read

To act on a group of cells they must first be selected. To select a cell, or group of cells use the selection arrow. This is shown when the cursor is placed near a left cell edge of a row (white) or the top of a column (black).

↱ Manoeuvres

1. In a new document, create a table **5** columns by **5** rows.

2. Select the first cell by moving near to its left edge and clicking the left mouse button when the arrow is displayed, as in the diagram.

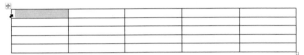

3. Move the mouse down and click again to remove the selection. Select the second column by moving near to the top edge of the column and clicking the mouse when the selection arrow is displayed.

4. Select the entire third row by double clicking when the arrow is displayed at the edge of any cell in the row or by clicking once when the arrow is in the selection bar on the left.

5. Select the nine cells in the middle of the table by clicking and dragging.

ℹ *To select cells, position the cursor within the required area then display the* **Layout** *tab and click the* **Select** *button,* [⬚ Select ▾] *in the* **Table** *group. Make the appropriate selection from the list which includes* **Select Table** *for the entire table.*

6. Close the document <u>without</u> saving.

Driving Lesson 74 - Changing the Column Width/Row Height

▣ Park and Read

The most important advantage of the tables feature over the tab stops is the ability to change the width of the column interactively. Note that the total width of the table is restricted by the space available between the margins. Reduce the width of small columns before widening others.

☞ Manoeuvres

1. Open the document **table**, created in **Driving Lesson 71** and saved in **Driving Lesson 72**.

2. Select the whole table and increase the font size to **16pt**.

3. If the ruler is not displayed, display the **View** tab and check **Ruler** in the **Show** group.

4. Click inside the table. When the insertion point is inside the table, the ruler shows the table column divides as symbols within the ruler.

5. A column width can be changed by clicking on the divide, then dragging to a new position before releasing the mouse button. A double-headed arrow appears when the mouse pointer is over the division.

6. Reduce the first three columns (make sure **Share Price** is on two lines).

7. Increase the width of the last column so that each entry of text fits on one row.

8. Select the **Layout** tab. Select the whole table and in the **Cell Size** group, use the spinner to change the **Table Row Height** to **1.5 cm**.

9. **Row Heights** can also be changed using the ruler. In **Print Layout** view, use the **Vertical Ruler**. Hold <**Alt**> whilst changing the row height to view the correct measurements on the ruler. Using this method, adjust the first row to a height if **1.65 cm**.

10. Save the document as **table1**.

11. Leave open for the next Driving Lesson.

Driving Lesson 75 - Inserting & Deleting Rows & Columns

🅿 Park and Read

It is possible to change the size of a table by adding or deleting rows and columns. Rows and columns can be added to or removed from the edges or the inside of the table, using the buttons in the **Rows & Columns** group of the **Layout** tab.

👌 Manoeuvres

1. Using the document **table1**, click in the table to display the **Layout** tab then place the cursor anywhere in the first column.

2. Click the **Insert Left** button, `⊞ Insert Left`, in the **Rows & Columns** group to insert one new column at the left edge of the table.

> ℹ️ *New rows can also be added to a table by placing the cursor in the last cell of the table and pressing <**Tab**>.*

3. With the column selected, use the **Numbering** button, `▤ ▾`, in the **Paragraph** group on the **Home** tab, to number the rows of text.

4. Make the column as small as possible, but ensure the numbers can be seen.

5. Widen the second column, using the symbols on the ruler. Place the cursor in the numbered row 2, and insert a new row above by clicking the **Insert Above** button from the **Layout** tab. The rows are automatically renumbered.

6. To delete the new row, select the row, click **Delete** from the **Rows and Columns** group on the **Layout** tab, then select **Delete Rows**.

7. Select the **Sector** column and insert a new column to the left.

8. Now delete this column. Make sure it is selected, then select **Delete** then **Delete Columns**.

9. Save the document with the same name.

10. Leave the document open.

> ℹ️ *Multiple cells that are next to each other in a row or column can be merged into a single cell by selecting them and then clicking **Merge Cells** button in the **Merge** group.*

Driving Lesson 76 - Table Borders/Shading

▣ Park and Read

The default border and lines applied to tables can be changed. Various types of lines, borders and shading can be added to an entire table, or to selected cells, rows or columns. There are also a number of predefined styles available.

↱ Manoeuvres

1. Use the document **table1**. Select the second row. Click the **Borders** button drop down on the **Design** tab of **Table Tools**. Select **Borders and Shading** from the menu. With the **Borders** tab displayed, make sure **All** is selected from **Setting**, select a double line from the **Style**.

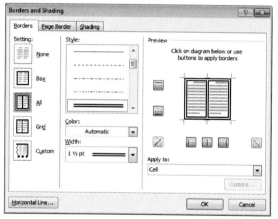

2. Click **OK**. Select the whole table and remove the lines by choosing **No Border** from the **Borders** button drop down menu.

3. Even with no borders there may still be faint **gridlines**, defining the table. If they are not shown click the **View Gridlines** from the **Borders** button drop down menu. These lines are for guidance only when working on the table, they do not print. To remove, click the **View Gridlines** option again.

i   *View Gridlines is a separate button on the **Layout** tab.*

4. Select a range of cells within the table and continue to experiment with different **Styles**. Try changing the **Color** and **Width** of the lines.

5. Select the first row. Use the **Borders** button to display the **Borders and Shading** dialog box. Select the **Shading** tab. Click on various squares within the **Fill** palette and observe the effects in the **Preview** panel. Select a **Fill** option and click **OK** to apply your chosen background colour to the cells.

6. Save the document using the same name and close it.

Driving Lesson 77 - Revision

This covers the features introduced in this section. Try not to refer to the preceding Driving Lessons while completing it.

1. Start a new document.

2. Create a table with **3** columns and **11** rows.

3. Enter the following headings in the columns: **Author**, **Title** and **Type**.

4. Open the document **books**.

5. Print a copy of the document, then close it.

6. Enter the information from the printout into the table.

7. Make all the headings bold.

8. Shade the background of the headings with **Dark Blue** and shade the rest of the cells with a light shade of **Green**.

9. Change the font of the headings to **Tahoma** (use an alternative font if this one is not available) and change the **Font Color** to **White**.

10. Centre all of the text in the table, take care to centre the text and not the table, and change the colour of the remaining text to **Bright Green**.

11. Save the table as **my table** and close it. Close the **books** document.

| i |

*Check the **Answers** section at the back of this guide for an indication of how your document should look.*

If you experienced any difficulty completing the Revision, refer back to the Driving Lessons in this section. Then redo the Revision.

Driving Lesson 78 - Revision

This covers the features introduced in this section. Try not to refer to the preceding Driving Lessons while completing it.

1. Start a new document.

2. Create a new table to match the table below, an invoice. You will need to use **Merge Cells**.

> *Multiple cells that are next to each other in a row or column can be merged into a single larger cell by selecting them and then clicking **Merge Cells** button in the **Merge** group of the **Table Tools Layout** tab.*

Invoice				
Ref No	Description	Qty	Price	Total
Subtotal				
VAT				
Total				

3. Save the document as **invoice** and close it.

4. Start a new document.

5. Create the following table with the text, lines and shading:

Date	Order Form	Terms	
Title	Type	Licence Number	Price
		Total	

6. Save the document as **order form**, then print a copy of the table.

7. To allow room for more orders, insert three new four-column rows into the main part of the table.

8. Save the changes and then close the document.

If you experienced any difficulty completing the Revision, refer back to the Driving Lessons in this section. Then redo the Revision.

Once you are confident with the features, complete the Record of Achievement Matrix referring to the section at the end of the guide. Only when competent move on to the next Section.

Section 10
Document Manipulation

By the end of this Section you should be able to:

Select Paper Size

Change Page Orientation

Change Margins

Insert Page Breaks

Apply Styles

To gain an understanding of the above features, work through the **Driving Lessons** in this **Section**.

For each **Driving Lesson**, read the **Park and Read** instructions, without touching the keyboard, then work through the numbered steps of the **Manoeuvres** on the computer. Complete the **Revision Exercise(s)** at the end of the section to test your knowledge.

Driving Lesson 79 - Document Setup

▣ Park and Read

The default paper size used by *Word* is **A4** but, because some situations call for the use of non-standard paper sizes, this can be changed. The size selected will depend upon both the printer and the particular application in use. Page **Orientation** can also be changed – a document can be printed in **Portrait** or **Landscape**.

Margins determine the distance between the text and the edges of the paper. The top and bottom margins are used for features such as headers, footers and page numbering. A large top margin can be set when working with headed notepaper. The top and bottom margins are, by default, set to 2.54cm.

Side margins can be changed to allow space for binding (**Gutter margin**), to change the length of the document and to improve its readability. By default, the side margins (left and right) are set at 2.54cm. *Word* has many predefined settings for page size and margins available.

⮐ Manoeuvres

1. Open the document **Retail**. At the beginning of the document type the words **Page Size 23cm x 18cm**. Press <**Enter**> twice.

2. Display the **Page Layout** tab and click the **Size** button, from the **Page Setup** group. Select **More Paper Sizes**.

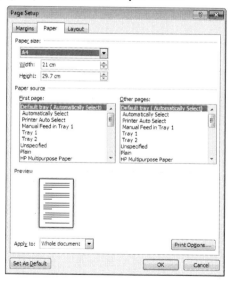

continued over

Driving Lesson 79 - Continued

3. Change the width to **18** cm and the height to **23** cm, either by editing the numbers or by using the up and down arrows. Note that the **Paper size** box has changed to **Custom size**. Click **OK**.

4. Preview the document. There are now 4 pages where there were 3 before. Close the preview and return the paper size to **A4** - using the **Size** button to select **A4**.

5. To change the **Orientation** of the document to landscape, click the **Orientation** button and select **Landscape**. Notice that the **Ruler** across the top of the page is now much longer.

6. Close the document <u>without</u> saving the changes.

7. Open the document **Scents**.

8. To change the document margins, display the **Page Layout** tab and click the **Margins** button.

9. Select **Custom Margins** option at the bottom of the list. The **Margins** tab is displayed in the **Page Setup** dialog box. The **Margins** settings are shown.

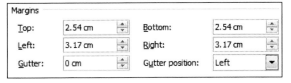

10. Increase the **Top**, **Bottom**, **Left** and **Right** margins to **5cm**, either by editing the numbers or by using the up and down arrows. Click **OK**.

11. Justify the text.

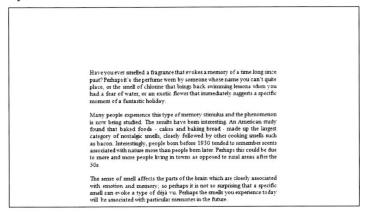

12. Print the document and close it <u>without</u> saving.

Driving Lesson 80 - Page Breaks

▣ Park and Read

It may be necessary to start a new page by choice. This is known as forcing a new page. Don't repeatedly use the **<Enter>** key to create a new page; it's good practice to insert a **page break**. If this is done in **Print Layout** view, a new page appears on the screen.

↱ Manoeuvres

1.   Open the document **Packages**.

2.   Position the cursor at the beginning of the second paragraph, display the **Page Layout** tab and click **Breaks**, then select **Page** under **Page Breaks**.

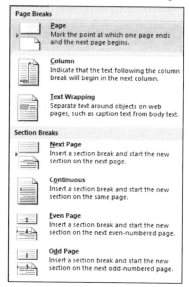

3.   A page break is inserted. Position the cursor at the beginning of the last paragraph. An alternative method to insert a break is to use a key press. Press **<Ctrl Enter>** to insert a page break.

4.   **Preview** the results. Use the **Zoom** button to view the 3 pages side-by-side. Click the **Home** tab to return to the document.

5.   To remove a page break click at the beginning of the page, after the break and press the **<Backspace>** key twice to delete it. Remove the page breaks to restore the document to a single page.

6.   Check that you have a one page document by checking the **Status Bar**, which displays **Page 1 of 1**.

7.   Close the document <u>without</u> saving.

Driving Lesson 81 - Styles

▣ Park and Read

Styles are pre-created formats consisting of paragraph and font formats. When they are applied, text will be formatted accordingly. Styles also ensure that formatting is consistent throughout a document.

↱ Manoeuvres

1. Open the document **Retail**.

2. Highlight the first heading, **Computers and Retailing**.

3. Display the **Home** tab and in the **Styles** group, click the **Heading 1** button. The formatting associated with this style is applied to the selected text.

   AaBbC(
   Heading 1

   > ### COMPUTERS AND RETAILING
   > Computers can assist in many of the functions of a retailing organisation. Among areas which can be assisted by computers are:
   >
   > 1) Item Identification and Customer receipts.
   >
   > 2) Stock Control and Re-ordering.
   >
   > 3) Customer Account Maintenance.

4. For **Styles** that do not appear in the **Style** group, use the up and down scroll buttons to display other rows.

   Previous row
   Next row
   More

5. Scroll through the document and highlight the heading **1. Item Identification**. Select the style **Subtitle** from the **Styles** group.

   > *1. Item Identification*
   > The traditional price ticket on items has been replace
   > can assist retailers by providing easy input of sales in
   >
   > Among the methods currently being employed are:-

6. Scroll through the document, formatting all numbered headings as **Subtitle**.

7. Highlight the text **A) Bar-Coding**.

   continued over

Driving Lesson 81 - Continued

8. The **More** button displays the **Quick Styles Galley** in full. Click the **More** button.

9. Apply the **List Paragraph** style. Change all the other lettered headings to the **List Paragraph** style.

10. A style can be applied to a paragraph of text. Select the first paragraph.

11. Choose the **Emphasis** style from the **Quick Styles Gallery**.

COMPUTERS AND RETAILING

Computers can assist in many of the functions of a retailing organisation. Among areas which can be assisted by computers are:

1) Item Identification and Customer receipts.

2) Stock Control and Re-ordering.

12. Scroll down the document until the **1. Item Identification** heading is displayed.

13. Double click the word **traditional** to select it. This ensures the style will only be applied to the word rather than the paragraph.

14. Select the **Strong** style to apply the style to the selected word only.

1. Item Identification

The **traditional** price ticket on items has been replaced by a variety of new methods which can assist retailers by providing easy input of sales information.

Among the methods currently being employed are:-

15. Preview the document.

16. Save the document as **styles** and then close it.

Driving Lesson 82 - Revision

This covers the features introduced in this section. Try not to refer to the preceding Driving Lessons while completing it.

1. Open the document **References**.

2. Take note of the number of pages the document contains.

3. Change the paper size to **Legal 21.59 cm x 35.56 cm**.

4. What happens to the number of pages?

5. Move to page **4** and insert a page break after the **Word Processing** paragraph, so that **Real-Time Systems** starts page **5**.

6. Preview the document and then close it <u>without</u> saving.

7. Open the document **Paper**.

8. Change the left and right margins to **5cm** and change the page orientation to **Landscape**.

9. Change all of the bold headings to **Heading 1**.

10. Change the first sentence after each heading to **Heading 2**.

11. Print preview the document.

12. Close the document <u>without</u> saving.

13. Open the document **headlines**.

14. Apply the style **Title** to all headings in the document.

15. Apply the style **Normal** to the rest of the text. Preview the document to see the effects of using the styles.

16. Change the orientation to landscape.

17. Change the margins to the **Narrow** style.

18. Preview the document.

19. Close the document <u>without</u> saving.

i   *Answers are shown in the **Answers** section at the end of this guide.*

If you experienced any difficulty completing the Revision, refer back to the Driving Lessons in this section. Then redo the Revision.

Once you are confident with the features, complete the Record of Achievement Matrix referring to the section at the end of the guide. Only when competent move on to the next Section.

Section 11
Mail Merge

By the end of this Section you should be able to:

Create a Main Document

Create a Data Source

Edit the Main Document

Perform Mail Merge

To gain an understanding of the above features, work through the **Driving Lessons** in this **Section**.

For each **Driving Lesson**, read the **Park and Read** instructions, without touching the keyboard, then work through the numbered steps of the **Manoeuvres** on the computer. Complete the **Revision Exercise(s)** at the end of the section to test your knowledge.

Driving Lesson 83 - Mail Merge

▣ Park and Read

The **Merge** feature is used to combine a **Main Document** (a letter, for example), with a separate list - the **Data Source** (names and addresses, for example), into one document. These two files, when merged, create a personalised copy of the document for everyone on the list. Mailing labels to the same group of people can be created, if required, using the same technique.

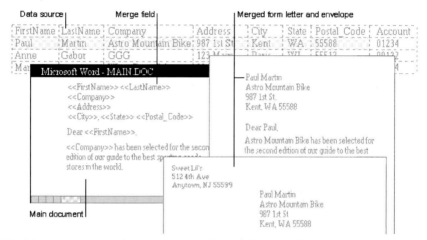

Two important terms that are used with merging are **Field** and **Record**. The following example shows **fields** (columns - Surname, First name, Street, Town, County) and **records** (rows - information for each person):

Surname	First name	Street	Town	County
Chapman	Ian	7 The Avenue	Boldon	Tyne & Wear
Peagram	Norma	5 St Georges	Morpeth	Northumberland

A **Data Source** is a document containing all the records used in a merged document in table format. These documents need a great deal of planning as they can be used for various applications.

It is best to break the information into as many fields as possible. For example, **Name** could be a field, but, **Surname**, **First Name** and **Initial** would be more useful, depending on requirements. **Paul French** entered in one field cannot be used in a merged document as **P French**, **Paul**, **Mr French** or **Mr P French**. Every record must have exactly the same number of fields, so some fields may have to be left blank.

Data Source files are used many times. As situations change, it will be necessary to add new records, change records and delete records. These changes can be made using the standard editing techniques.

Driving Lesson 84 - Creating the Main Document

P Park and Read

The first step in mail merging is to create the **Main Document** to form the basis for the merge. A main document can take a range of formats, such as form letters, mailing labels, envelopes or catalogues. *Word* gives a great deal of assistance in the form of the **Step by Step Mail Merge Wizard**. This comprises six steps that define the complete **Mail Merge** process. You can move back and forth through the steps by using the **Next** and **Previous** links.

↱ Manoeuvres

1.   Create a new document.

2.   Display the **Mailings** tab and click the **Start Mail Merge** button.

3.   Select **Step by Step Mail Merge Wizard**. The **Mail Merge Task Pane** is displayed.

4.   Make sure **Letters** is selected from the **Select document type** list.

continued over

Driving Lesson 84 - Continued

5. Click [➡ Next: Starting document] to move to step 2.

6. At step 2 choose to **Use the current document**.

7. The main document can now be created. Display the **Insert** tab and on the first line of the blank document, enter the current date, using the **Date and Time** button, [📅 Date & Time], in the **Text** group.

8. From the **Available formats**, select the date in the format **17 April 2010**. Click **OK**.

9. Add 2 blank lines. Type the following paragraph.

    Dear

    This is just a brief reminder that the next annual conference of the Word Users' Club is only a few weeks away. Delegates are limited to 1500 this year, so please hurry and reserve your place!

    Sincerely

    Ms M S Word

10. Save the document with the name **main**.

[i] *The writing of the main document can be left until step 4 of the wizard, if required.*

11. Click [➡ Next: Select recipients] to move to step 3.

12. Leave the document open.

Driving Lesson 85 - Creating a Data Source

▣ Park and Read

An **Address List (Data Source)** can be used with any number of **Main Documents**, so its creation must be well thought out. It can be created before or after the main document and can be accessed at any time once created.

⌐ Manoeuvres

1. There is an option here to use an existing list but for now select **Type a new list** then click [🖳 Create...] .

2. Click the **Customize Columns** button to edit the field names. At the dialog box, remove field names so that only **Title**, **Last Name**, **Company Name**, **Address Line 1**, **Address Line 2** and **City** remain. Do this by clicking on each field name that is not needed and then **Delete**, selecting **Yes** at the prompt.

3. Click **Add** to add a new field. Type **Initial** into the box provided and click **OK**. Move it to the appropriate place in the list, above **Last Name** using the **Move Up** button. The field list is complete, click on **OK**.

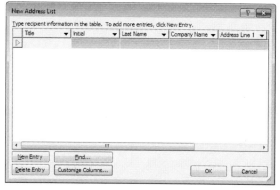

4. Using the **<Tab>** key to move from field to field, enter your own details and those of **3** other people (fictional if necessary). Select **New Entry** after each record. Click **OK** to finish.

5. When the **Save Address List** dialog box appears, save it to the **3 Word Processing** folder (or another folder if applicable), with the **File name** of **data**. The data is saved as a **Microsoft Office Address List** file (*.mdb).

6. The **Mail Merge Recipients** dialog box appears. The data source can be edited here at any time. Click **OK** to close it without making any changes.

7. Click [⇒ Next: Write your letter] to move on to step 4.

Driving Lesson 86 - Editing the Main Document

▣ Park and Read

After the fields have been decided, they can be incorporated into the **Main Document**.

↱ Manoeuvres

1. Add **2** blank lines at the top of the main document, the letter created earlier.

2. Place the cursor at the top of the document and click the drop down arrow on the **Insert Merge Field**.

3. Select **Title** from the **Fields** list. The field is added to the letter, **<<Title>>**.

4. Add a space in the document after the **Title** field, then click the **Insert Merge Field** button. Click **Initial**. Complete the fields as below (Remember to add spaces where necessary or press **<Enter>** to move to the next line).

    <<Title>> <<Initial>> <<Last Name>>
    <<Company Name>>
    <<Address Line 1>>
    <<Address Line 2>>
    <<City>>

ℹ️ *Adding a standard address block like the one above can be made easier by using the **Address block** option in the **Task Pane**.*

5. After **Dear** in the main part of the document, insert a space then the **Title** field followed by another space and then **Last Name**.

6. Save the document under the same name, **main** and leave it open.

Driving Lesson 87 - Merging

🅿 Park and Read

The hardest part of mail merge is the creation of the main and data source documents. It is easy to merge the two files. After the merge, you can print the merged letters. You can also save them as a separate file, if you want to use them again.

↱ Manoeuvres

1. Click 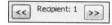 in the **Task Pane** to move to step **5** where the merged letters can be previewed and printed.

2. Use the chevrons near the top of the **Task Pane** to move through the final letters.

    <<   Recipient: 1   >>

ℹ️ *There are options on the **Mail Merge** task pane to edit the recipients list (the data source) or to individually exclude any particular letter from the merge.*

3. Click ⇨ Next: Complete the merge to complete the merge.

4. Read the information in the **Mail Merge** task pane then click 🖨 Print... to select letters for printing.

5. Make sure **All** is selected from the **Merge to Printer** dialog box and click **OK**.

6. The merged letters can all be printed by clicking **OK**, but if you wish to save paper, click **Cancel**.

7. To save the merged file, click 📝 Edit individual letters... in the task pane.

8. In the **Merge to New Document** dialog box, select **All** and click **OK**. A document is opened containing all the individual letters produced by the merge. Personal messages could now be added to the letters.

9. Save the file as **merge** and close all documents, saving any changes if prompted.

Driving Lesson 88 - Open a Data Source

Park and Read

You don't always have to create a data source from scratch. Existing data source files can be used when performing mail merge.

Manoeuvres

1.   Open the document **main** (click **Yes** at the prompt to include data).

If the data is not included, the sequence of steps in this lesson will be different.

2.   Display the **Mailings** tab, click **Start Mail Merge** and select **Step by Step Mail Merge Wizard**.

3.   As this is already a main document the **Mail Merge** should start at step **3**, **Select recipients**. Under **Use an existing list** select

   ⊞ Select a different list...

4.   In the **Select Data Source** dialog box, locate and display the location of the supplied data files. Select **Client** from the list of files and click **Open**.

5.   The **Invalid Merge Field** dialog box appears.

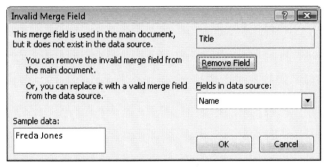

6.   This suggests that the fields on the letter are not found in the source data. The dialog box allows fields to be removed from the letter or linked to a different source field. Drop down the **Fields in data source** list. There are only 4 fields in the data source and these must be linked to the letter.

7.   The **Title** field does not appear in the **Client** source data. Click Remove Field. Also remove the **Initial** field. The next field on the letter is **Last_Name** and this can be linked to the **Name** field in **Client**. Click **OK**.

continued over

Driving Lesson 88 - Continued

8.   **Company_Name** is the next field on the letter and it can be linked to **Company** in **Clients**. Drop down the list, select **Company** and then **OK**.

9.   Link **Address_Line_1** to **Street**, remove **Address_Line_2** and link **City** to **Town**. Remove the second **Title** field and link the second **Last Name** field to **Name**.

10.   Click **OK** in the **Mail Merge Recipient** dialog box

11.   Click on [➡ Next: Write your letter], if the main document requires editing, add any new fields from the **Client** data source, if required. Preview the letters before closing all documents <u>without</u> saving.

12.   The mail merge feature also makes it easy to create labels for your mass mailing. Start a new document and display the **Mailings** tab. To create labels click on **Start Mail Merge** and select **Labels**.

13.   At the dialog box, choose the label - Label vendor **Avery A4/A5** and Product number **C2160** (a 7x3 A4 sheet of labels). Click **OK**.

14.   Click on the **Select Recipients** button and select the **Use Existing List** option, then navigate to the supplied data folder and select **Client**.

15.   Choose [Address Block]. Click the [Match Fields...] button to link the fields. This is so that *Word* can recognise which fields are to be included in the Block.

16.   Note that *Word* has recognised that **Last Name** and **Name** match, as do the two **Company** fields.

17.   Drop down the **Address 1** list and select **Street**, similarly select **Town** from the **City** list. Click **OK** then click **OK** again after checking the preview.

18.   The **Address Block** field needs to be applied to all other labels. Click [🗐 Update Labels].

19.   **Preview** the results [Preview Results], then **Finish and Merge** [Finish & Merge ▾]. Select to **Edit Individual Documents**, to save paper, otherwise **Print Documents**. In either case, select which records to merge, before selecting **OK**.

20.   Close all documents <u>without</u> saving.

Driving Lesson 89 - Revision

This covers the features introduced in this section. Try not to refer to the preceding Driving Lessons while completing it.

1.   Create a short letter, which is to be the main document, informing a company of a visit, using the following text:

      Dear

      Just to confirm our visit to your company on   regarding a health and safety inspection.

      Yours sincerely

      Janet Orr

      Cleaning Inspector

2.   Save the main document as **main letter**.

3.   Create a data source file with **4** records containing the field names **Title**, **Last Name**, **Company Name**, **Address Line 1**, **City** and **Date**.

4.   Save this as **data source** in the **3 Word Processing** data folder.

5.   Insert the merge field names in the appropriate places in the main document.

6.   Merge the two files and print a copy of the four letters, saving the merged document as **merged2**.

7.   Close all open documents <u>without</u> saving.

8.   Open the document **Buslet**; this is a prepared mail merge letter.

9.   Display the **Mailings** tab and select **Client.docx** as the **Recipients** file.

10.   Use the **Edit Recipient List** button to view the data attached.

11.   Click on **OK** to return to the **Main Document**.

12.   Use the **Finish & Merge** button to merge to a new document and prepare the individual letters. Preview the letters.

13.   Close all documents <u>without</u> saving.

If you experienced any difficulty completing the Revision, refer back to the Driving Lessons in this section. Then redo the Revision.

Driving Lesson 90 - Revision

This covers the features introduced in this section. Try not to refer to the preceding Driving Lessons while completing it.

1.   Start a new document and create a mail merge letter from the **current document**.

2.   Edit the main document by inserting the date (first format) and typing the following letter:

    Dear

    I am planning a party for the ghosts of great naval explorers, to be held on board my ship, the Mary Rose, in the Solent. Please arrive in your own vessel, the   and a rowing boat will transfer you to the party. I look forward to seeing through you.

    Sincerely

    Henry VIII

3.   Save the main document as **explorers**.

4.   Create a data source document containing these fields: **First Name, Last Name, Country** and **Vessel**.

5.   Save this document as **shipping list** and add the following records:

Christopher	**Columbus**	**Spain**	**Santa Maria**
Francis	**Drake**	**England**	**Golden Hind**
James	**Cook**	**England**	**Endeavour**

6.   Add these fields to the top of the main document:

    <<First Name>> <<Last Name>>
    <<Country>>

7.   After **Dear** add **<<First Name>>** and after **your own vessel, the** add **<<Vessel>>**.

8.   Remove any surplus space if necessary.

9.   Save the document under the same name.

10. Merge to a new document, add your name to the header and print the document. Close the merged documents <u>without</u> saving.

11. Close all documents, saving, if prompted.

If you experienced any difficulty completing the Revision, refer back to the Driving Lessons in this section. Then redo the Revision.

Once you are confident with the features, complete the Record of Achievement Matrix referring to the section at the end of the guide. Only when competent move on to the next Section.

Section 12
Objects

By the end of this Section you should be able to:

Insert Drawn Objects

Insert a Picture

Insert an Image from File

Insert Charts

Move and Resize a Picture, Image or Chart

Cut and Paste Objects

To gain an understanding of the above features, work through the **Driving Lessons** in this **Section**.

For each **Driving Lesson**, read the **Park and Read** instructions, without touching the keyboard, then work through the numbered steps of the **Manoeuvres** on the computer. Complete the **Revision Exercise(s)** at the end of the section to test your knowledge.

Driving Lesson 91 - Drawn Objects

▣ Park and Read

Objects include anything that can be imported or drawn onto a page; a table, a picture a chart or a drawn object. They can all be moved around a page in a similar manner, with text wrapping around, as required.

Word has numerous shapes and lines that can be drawn directly onto a page. They can be filled with solid or opaque colours, textures or pictures, with options for a different coloured border. There is a variety of shapes that can be used in flowcharts and callouts.

⌒ Manoeuvres

1. Start a new document and select the **Insert** tab.

2. From the **Illustrations** group, select the **Shapes** button. A variety of shapes is shown.

3. From **Rectangles**, select the first **Rectangle**. The cursor becomes a cross hair on the page.

4. Click and drag a rectangle shape. Once the mouse button is released the shape is drawn and handles appear on each side and in the corners.

ℹ *Notice that once a shape is drawn the **Drawing Tools Format** tab becomes available.*

5. Click and drag the bottom right corner down to the right to increase the size of the rectangle.

6. At the top of the rectangle is a green handle. Move the mouse over it. It becomes **Rotate**, ↺.

7. Drag the handle to the right slightly. The rectangle turns about the centre.

8. From **Shape Styles** select the supplied style, **Coloured Fill - Black**.

9. The shape is coloured. Click the **More** button from **Shape Styles** to reveal more options. Select red square on row 4 – **Subtle Effect – Red, Accent 2**.

continued over

Driving Lesson 91 - Continued

10. Try other types of styles.

11. From the **Insert Shapes** group, select an oval and draw the shape away from the rectangle, whilst holding down <**Shift**>. The shape will be symmetrical, i.e. a circle. (The same method used on a rectangle will produce a square.)

12. Select the drop down arrow of **Shape Fill** button, ⬛ Shape Fill ▾ from **Shape Styles**.

13. Select **Light Blue** from **Standard Colors**.

14. With the circle still selected, the **Shape Outline** drop down, ✏ Shape Outline ▾.

15. Select **Dark Red** from **Standard Colors**. The circle now has a thin dark red border.

16. With the circle still selected, click the **Shape Styles** dialog box launcher. The **Format Shape** dialog box is displayed. Many changes can now be made at once.

17. Change the **Transparency** to about **75%** by moving the slider.

18. Change the **Style** of the line to a **4½ pt** double line. Click **Close**.

19. Place the cursor in the middle of the circle. It changes to a four headed arrow. Drag the circle over a corner of the rectangle. It should be visible through the circle.

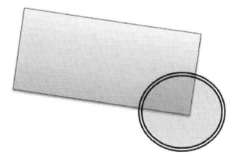

20. Experiment with other shapes and other effects, such as **Shadows** and **3D**.

21. Close the document <u>without</u> saving.

Driving Lesson 92 - Inserting a Picture

▣ Park and Read

Any picture or graphic stored on the computer or available online can be placed at the insertion point on a document. *Word* is supplied with many pictures in the **Clip Art** folder. Other graphics, from other programs can also be incorporated into documents – providing they are in a format that *Word* can import.

⌐ Manoeuvres

1. Start a new document, and type the text **Here is a picture**, followed by a space.

2. Display the **Insert** tab and click **Clip Art** in the **Illustrations** group.

3. The **Clip Art** task pane is displayed. Type **animals** in the **Search for** box and click **Go**.

4. A number of relevant images will be displayed in the task pane, (there may be a slight delay as they load). Select the clip of the **Tiger** (or an alternative if this is not available) by clicking on it. It will be inserted into the document as part of the text line.

5. The handles appear around the image to indicate it is selected, if not click on the picture to select it. The **Picture Tools, Format** tab will be displayed.

continued over

Driving Lesson 92 - Continued

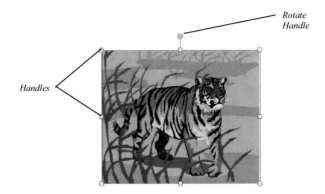

Rotate Handle

Handles

ℹ️ *By default the picture is in line with the text and cannot be moved independently, but this can be changed (covered in a later Driving Lesson).*

6. With the picture still selected, press **<Delete>** to remove it.

7. There should be a large selection of pictures in clipart. Spend some time searching for and viewing pictures from various categories.

ℹ️ *A star ⬛, at the bottom right of a clip indicates it is an animated clip. This type of clip, however, is not animated in Word.*

8. Close the **Clip Art** task pane, using its **Close** button, ⊠.

9. To insert an image from file, click at the end of the text to place the cursor, display the **Insert** tab and click **Picture** in the **Illustrations** group.

10. In the **Insert Picture** dialog box, display the location of the supplied data files and select the **cat** file.

11. Click **Insert**. The image is inserted in the document.

12. To select the image and display the handles, click on it.

13. Delete the **cat** image by pressing **<Delete>**.

14. Close the document <u>without</u> saving.

Driving Lesson 93 - Inserting Charts

▣ Park and Read

A chart can be added to a document to display information professionally. This could be useful when producing a report containing figures, because sometimes a visual representation of figures can help to make them easier to understand.

↻ Manoeuvres

1. Start a new document. Display the **Insert** tab and click the **Chart** button in the **Illustrations** group.

2. Select a **Clustered Column** chart type and click **OK**. A sample chart will appear in the document, with the datasheet, an *Excel* worksheet, visible on the right.

	A	B	C	D	E	F	G
1		Series 1	Series 2	Series 3			
2	Category 1	4.3	2.4	2			
3	Category 2	2.5	4.4	2			
4	Category 3	3.5	1.8	3			
5	Category 4	4.5	2.8	5			
6							
7							
8		To resize chart data range, drag lower right corner of range.					

3. In the datasheet, position the mouse over **Series 1** and click. Type in **Jan**. Press <Tab> to move to the next column and enter **Feb**. Press <Tab> again and enter **Mar**. Click in **E1** and enter **Apr**.

4. Using the above process enter the following information:

	Jan	Feb	Mar	Apr
Word	200	150	175	190
Access	300	250	300	50
Excel	220	150	100	275

5. Remove the **Category 4** row data by selecting the whole row and deleting it. Make sure there is no blank row inside the blue border. Drag the blue border upwards if necessary, by its bottom right corner.

6. Close the *Excel* window, to remove the datasheet and view the chart.

7. Save the document as **objects** and leave it open for the next Driving Lesson.

▣ *Click the chart at any time to select it and display the **Chart Tools Design** tab, then click the **Edit Data** button, to display and edit the datasheet in Excel.*

Driving Lesson 94 - Move and Resize Objects

Park and Read

Pictures and any other objects can be moved around, if they are floating. Just click and drag! Resizing is slightly more difficult. After the object is selected, handles are displayed. By clicking and dragging a handle it is possible to make the object larger or smaller.

Manoeuvres

1. Use the document **objects** created in the previous Driving Lesson.

2. To make sure the chart is selected, click on it once. **Chart** handles are slightly different from other handles in that they are contained within the object border and are denoted as dots.

3. Select the bottom right corner of the chart and click and drag in towards the middle of the chart to decrease the size of the chart.

i *Dragging the middle handles of an object will deform the shape, i.e. stretch or squash it. Dragging the corner handles of any object can change its height <u>and</u> width.*

i *For charts and drawn shapes, holding down <Shift> while dragging a corner handle will change the size but keeps the relative dimensions the same, i.e. a square will still be square.*

4. To make it possible to move an object, its text wrapping properties must be amended. Display the **Format** tab, click the **Wrap Text** button and select **Square**. Move the mouse over a blank part of the chart or its border. The cursor changes to ✛ when it is in a position to move it.

5. Click and drag the chart to a different position on the page and click away from it to deselect it.

6. In the same document, use the **Clip Art** button on the **Insert** tab. Search for **cars**, and insert a clip on the page.

7. While it is still selected (it may be partially obscured by the chart), click the **Wrap Text** button on the **Format** tab and select **Square**.

continued over

Driving Lesson 94 - Continued

8. Click and drag the picture (use the ✛ cursor) to another position away from the chart.

9. Make sure the picture still has handles visible, i.e. it is selected. Move the pointer over one of the corner handles (the mouse pointer changes).

10. Click and drag inwards to make the picture smaller or outwards to make the picture larger.

> *For an image or picture, dragging a corner handle will always maintain the correct relative dimensions, there is no need to hold down <**Shift**>.*

11. Demonstrate the difference between resizing with the corner handles and with the middle handles.

12. Finally make the image about half its original size.

13. Select the **Insert** tab and click **Picture**, [Picture] The **Insert Picture** dialog box is displayed.

14. Locate the supplied data files, select the image **cat** and click **Insert**.

15. To be able to move the image, click the **Wrap Text** button on the **Format** tab and select **Square**.

16. Click and drag the cat to the top right corner of the page.

17. If the cat obscures the chart, move the chart out of the way.

18. Use a corner handle to resize it, making it half its original size.

19. Save **objects** using the same name.

20. Open the document **Golf**.

21. Use clip art to locate a golf picture and insert it on the page. Resize the picture smaller if it's a large image.

22. Click on the [Position ▾] drop down arrow. Move the cursor around the options to move the picture around the page. Select one of the options and click the mouse button. This automatically makes the text wrap square.

23. Experiment, before closing the document <u>without</u> saving.

24. Leave **objects** open.

Driving Lesson 95 - Copy and Paste Objects

▣ Park and Read

Objects such as images and charts can be copied to a different location within a document or to a different document. When an object is copied the original is unchanged.

↱ Manoeuvres

1.   Using the document **objects**, select the chart.

2.   Click the **Copy** button, [⧉], on the **Home** tab or use the key press <**Ctrl C**> to copy the chart. Click away from the chart.

3.   Click **Paste**, [📋], or use the key press <**Ctrl V**> to paste a copy of the original on top of the first chart.

4.   Make the copy about half its original size and drag it to a blank area of the page.

ℹ️ *Take care to click in the **Chart Area** before attempting to move a chart. The **Plot Area** will move the chart within the confines of the **Chart Area**, i.e. inside the chart borders.*

5.   Select the original chart.

6.   Press <**Delete**> to delete it.

ℹ️ *Pictures and images are deleted in the same way.*

7.   Copy the picture of the **car** and move it away from the original.

8.   Paste the copy of the **picture** into the current document.

9.   Start a new document and paste the **car** picture into it.

10. Insert the **cat** image from the data files into the new document.

11. Copy the **cat** and then click away from it to deselect it.

12. Paste the **cat** into the same document.

13. Use the **Taskbar** to display the **objects** document.

14. Paste the **cat** image into this document.

15. Copy the **chart** and paste it into the other open document (unsaved).

16. Leave the documents open for the next exercise.

Driving Lesson 96 - Cut and Paste Objects

▣ Park and Read

Objects such as images and charts can be removed from their original location and pasted to a different location within a document or in a different document. When an object is cut the original is removed.

⌒ Manoeuvres

1. Using the same documents as in the previous Driving Lesson, select a **cat** image from the unsaved document.

2. Click **Cut**, ⌙✂⌐, or use the key press <**Ctrl X**> to cut the image to remove it ready to be placed elsewhere.

3. Click **Paste**, ▭, or use the key press <**Ctrl V**> to paste the cat back into the document.

4. Select the **cat** and cut it again.

5. Switch to the **objects** document.

6. Paste the **cat** into this document, making sure nothing else is selected.

7. Move to the other, unsaved document.

8. Cut the **car** and then paste it back into the same document.

9. Cut the **chart** and paste it back into the same document.

10. Display the **Clipboard** pane.

11. Cut the remaining objects from this document and paste them in the **objects** document using the **Clipboard**.

12. Save **objects** and close it.

13. Close the other document, <u>without</u> saving.

14. Empty the **Clipboard** and close it.

Driving Lesson 97 - Revision

This covers the features introduced in this section. Try not to refer to the preceding Driving Lessons while completing it.

1. Start a new document.

2. Insert a **Clip Art** picture of your choice from any **Collection**.

3. Delete the picture.

4. Insert a different image from **Clip Art**.

5. Move the picture to the centre of the page.

6. Resize the picture to make it larger.

7. Create a header and add your name to it.

8. Print one copy of the document.

9. Close the document <u>without</u> saving.

10. Open the document **cat**.

11. Position the cursor at the end of the paragraph finishing with **stalked off** and start a new line.

12. Insert the picture **cat** from the data files.

13. Resize the picture to about half its original size.

14. Add your name and the date to the footer.

15. Preview the document.

16. Close the document <u>without</u> saving.

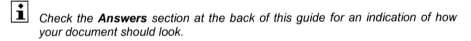 *Check the **Answers** section at the back of this guide for an indication of how your document should look.*

If you experienced any difficulty completing the Revision, refer back to the Driving Lessons in this section. Then redo the Revision.

Once you are confident with the features, complete the Record of Achievement Matrix referring to the section at the end of the guide.

Answers

Driving Lesson 6

Step 8 a) **Show/Hide** (**Home** tab)

b) **Save** (on the **Quick Access Toolbar**)

c) **Theme Colors** (**Page Layout** tab)

d) **Spelling and Grammar** (**Review** tab)

e) **Format Painter** (**Home** tab)

f) **Bold** (**Home** tab)

g) **Insert Table of Authorities** (**References** tab)

h) **Numbering** (**Home** tab)

Step 9 **Format** tab (which is only available when a picture is selected)

Driving Lesson 7

Step 2 **Mailings**

Step 3 Press **F1** key

Step 7 Green squiggly underline

Step 8 On the **Insert** tab, **Pages** group, click **Cover Page**. Click a cover page layout from the gallery of options

Driving Lesson 27

Step 5 The blank area to the left of the document is the **Selection Bar**

Driving Lesson 31

Step 1 The **Print** screen is displayed

Step 2 The normal setting is **Print All Pages**

Step 3 The normal setting for the **Copies** is **1**

Step 4 **Print Preview** shows the layout of the document as it will be printed

Step 13 The document contains **3** pages

Driving Lesson 32

Step 14 Enter **1,3** in the **Pages** box in **Settings** within the **Print** screen

Driving Lesson 41

Step 1 a) **B** switches **Bold** formatting on or off

b) **I** switches **Italic** formatting on or off

c) **U** switches **Underline** formatting on or off

Step 2 A **Font** is a type or style of print.

Driving Lesson 52

Step 1 **11** possible spelling mistakes are highlighted in the document

Step 8 There are **5** matches

Step 12 There are **10** possible spelling mistakes indicated within the document

Driving Lesson 77

Author	Title	Type
Jane Austen	Pride and Prejudice	Prose
William Shakespeare	Macbeth	Drama
William Shakespeare	Othello	Drama
Thomas Hardy	Jude the Obscure	Prose
Christina Rossetti	Goblin Market	Poetry
William Blake	The Tyger	Poetry
Christopher Marlowe	Doctor Faustus	Drama
Charles Dickens	Great Expectations	Prose
Charlotte Brönte	Jane Eyre	Prose
George Eliot	The Mill on the Floss	Prose

Driving Lesson 82

Step 4   The number of pages is reduced to 5

Driving Lesson 97

Spells

Wanda, the wicked witch of Wolverhampton, sat in her cave one gloomy winter's morning and watched the rain outside.

"What a glorious day, Pyewacket!" she exclaimed to her cat who was curled up on a pile of dead leaves. Pyewacket simply glared at Wanda for a whole minute, then got up and stalked off.

"Suit yourself, you miserable old moggy!" yelled Wanda, throwing a jar of eye of newt in the direction of the retreating feline.

Wanda pondered how she would spend the day, now that Pyewacket was in a huff. She picked up her book of spells, which was in the corner and began to leaf through the pages. One spell caught her eye: "Ungrateful Cat Concoction."

"Hmm" said Wanda, "this could be interesting. What ingredients do I need?"

She read through the list, which contained the following items:

Warts

Pythons' tongues (2)

Bat's liver (1)

3 hairs from the offending cat

Wanda followed the recipe carefully and soon her cauldron was bubbling furiously. She retrieved the cat from his hiding place and hurried to throw him into the magic stew. Unfortunately for Wanda, Pyewacket knew exactly what she intended to do and began to spit and claw. His mistress, half-blinded by the furious cat, overbalanced and fell into the cauldron.

Wanda was instantaneously turned into a mouse. She managed to scramble out of the cauldron, but Pyewacket was waiting. And he was hungry...

A.N. Other 14 June 2010

Glossary

Alignment	Where text appears on the page in relation to the margins.
Application	A software program such as *Word*.
Copy & Paste	Duplicate text or images, etc. from one place to another within a document or between documents.
Cut & Paste	Remove text or images, etc. from one place and place them in another.
First Line Indent	Move the first line further in from the left margin than the others in a paragraph.
Font	A type or style of print.
Format	Change the way a document looks.
Headers & Footers	Common identification lines at the top and/or bottom of each page.
HTML	The format of web pages.
Justified	Straight left and right margins.
Orientation	The way up a page is - **Portrait** or **Landscape**.
Mail Merge	Combining a main document with a data source.
Print Preview	A feature that shows how a document will look before it is printed.
Save	Keep a copy of your file on the hard disk, memory stick or floppy disk.
Selection Bar	A blank area at the left of the page, used to select text.
Styles	Pre-created formats consisting of paragraph and font formats.
Symbols	Special characters that are not on the keyboard.
Tabs	A precise measurement for aligning vertical rows of text.
Template	A base document that contains certain elements and can be used over and over again.
Undo & Redo	Features that allow you to reverse or reapply your last actions.
Web Page	Storage facility of internet information.
Word Wrap	How the computer automatically detects the end of a line and starts a new one.
Zoom	A feature that either allows the document to be viewed more closely, or more of the document, but in less detail.

Index

Record of Achievement Matrix

This Matrix is to be used to measure your progress while working through the guide. This is a learning reinforcement process, you judge when you are competent.

Tick boxes are provided for each feature. 1 is for no knowledge, 2 some knowledge and 3 is for competent. A section is only complete when column 3 is completed for all parts of the section.

For details on sitting ECDL Examinations in your country please contact the local ECDL Licensee or visit the European Computer Driving Licence Foundation Limited web site at http://www.ecdl.org.

Tick the Relevant Boxes **1**: No Knowledge **2**: Some Knowledge **3**: Competent

Section	No.	Driving Lesson	1	2	3
1 Getting Started	1	Starting Word			
	2	Layout of the Word Screen			
	3	The Ribbon			
	4	The Quick Access Toolbar			
	5	Help			
2 Documents	8	Entering Text			
	9	Saving Documents			
	10	Closing a Document/Word			
	11	Creating a New Document			
	12	Open an Existing Document			
	13	Views			
	14	Saving in a Different Format			
	15	Save as a Template			
3 Editing Text	19	Inserting and Deleting Text			
	20	Select Words and Sentences			
	21	Select Lines and Paragraphs			
	22	Symbols			
	23	Undo and Redo			
	24	Show/Hide Characters			
	25	Soft Carriage Returns			
4 Printing	29	Previewing a Document			
	30	Printing a Document			
5 Formatting Text	33	Underline, Bold and Italic			
	34	Formatting of Selected Text			
	35	Fonts and Text Size			
	36	Changing Text Appearance			
	37	Subscript and Superscript			
	38	Changing Case			
	39	Format Painter			
	40	Cut, Copy and Paste			
6 Tools	45	Spelling Checker			
	46	Add to Dictionary			
	47	Hyphenation			
	48	Searching a Document			
	49	Replace			
	50	Zoom Control			
	51	Preferences			

Tick the Relevant Boxes **1**: No Knowledge **2**: Some Knowledge **3**: Competent

Section	No.	Driving Lesson	1	2	3
7 Formatting Paragraphs	54	Alignment			
	55	Indenting Paragraphs			
	56	Advanced Indentation			
	57	Bullets and Numbering			
	58	Line Spacing			
	59	Spacing Between Paragraphs			
	60	Tab Settings			
	61	Tab Alignment			
	62	Adding Borders			
8 Multiple Documents	65	Switch Between Documents			
	66	Cut, Copy, Paste Between Documents			
	67	Headers and Footers			
	68	Page Numbering			
9 Tables	71	Tables			
	72	Entering Text			
	73	Selecting Cells			
	74	Changing Column Width/Row Height			
	75	Inserting and Deleting Rows/Columns			
	76	Table Borders/Shading			
10 Document Manipulation	79	Document Setup			
	80	Page Breaks			
	81	Styles			
11 Mail Merge	83	Mail Merge			
	84	Creating the Main Document			
	85	Creating a Data Source			
	86	Editing the Main Document			
	87	Merging			
	88	Open a Data Source			
12 Objects	91	Drawn Objects			
	92	Inserting a Picture			
	93	Inserting Charts			
	94	Move and Resize Objects			
	95	Copy and Paste Objects			
	96	Cut and Paste Objects			

Other Products from CiA Training

CiA Training is a leading publishing company which has consistently delivered the highest quality products since 1985. Our experienced in-house publishing team has developed a wide range of flexible and easy to use self-teach resources for individual learners and corporate clients all over the world.

At the time of publication, we currently offer approved ECDL materials for:

- **ECDL Syllabus 5.0**

- **ECDL Syllabus 5.0 Revision Series**

- **ECDL Advanced Syllabus 2.0**

- **ECDL Advanced Syllabus 2.0 Revision Series**

Previous syllabus versions are also available upon request.

We hope you have enjoyed using this guide and would love to hear your opinions about our materials. To let us know how we're doing, and to get up to the minute information on our current range of products, please visit us at:

www.ciatraining.co.uk